Forty-five

is the New

Twenty-five

Forty-five is the New Twenty-five

Live like your best years are still ahead

Steven Sharp, M.Ed.

A.L.P.S. PRESS

For information regarding permission to reprint material from this book, please mail or email your request to:

Steven Sharp at ssharpga@me.com
www.45isthenew25.com

Author: Steven Sharp
Project Direction: Bonnie Daneker of Write Advisors, LLC
Book Cover Design: Lee Breed, Breed Design
Front and Back Cover Photos: Jen Baggett Photography
Copy editing: Melissa Heffner, Second Look Services

ISBN 978-0-9896495-0-6
1. Inspiration. 2. Self-Help. 3. Biography.
Manufactured in the United States of America
Printed in the United States of America by:
BookLogix, Alpharetta, GA

iTunes is a registered trademark of Apple, Inc.
Livescribe® is a registered trademark of Livescribe, Inc.
Logitech® is a registered trademark of Logitech, Inc.
Fitbit® is a registered trademark of Fitbit, Inc.

∞This paper meets the requirements of ANSI/NISO Z39.48-1992 (Permanence of Paper)

To my loving family

who has always encouraged me to be myself

and accepted me as I am.

Table of Contents

About this Book

All characters in this book are real except for Amelia O'Connor, Michele DiFranco and Aara Parkour. Their characters are real; their names are not. All events in this book are actual events.

This book uses certain graphic conventions to indicate different modes of communication and the variety of ways Steven attempts to capture the details of his life. These conventions are described here.

I AM SO EXCITED!!	Text message Steven sends.
What are you so excited about? Give me a call in a little bit after the kids have gone to bed.	Text message Steven receives.
	Indicates music, lyrics, or a song Steven uses to influence his mood or explain what he is thinking or feeling.
	Livescribe® notebook. The Livescribe® pen is a device that records sound and associates it with what is written when the sound occurs.
	Logitech® wireless headset. Allows for speech to text recognition for book dictation, listening to music, Skyping® with friends while doing household chores.
 novateur	This icon indicates the "Coaching Prep Form" Steven completes before each coaching session.
	Fitbit®. A device that tracks your daily steps and syncs wirelessly to various fitness apps. Used in the book to indicate Steven's exercise progress.

Introduction

Do you have fading dreams, or dreams you don't dare yourself to dream? Are you over forty or over forty-five and you believe the best years of your life are behind you? Is your life filled with naysayers, people telling you all the reasons you can't do something, that the best years of your life are behind you? If so, you are not alone: for a long time this was my life, too.

Maybe you jumped from career to career, industry to industry without ever being passionate about what you do for work. Or perhaps you want to change careers or re-enter the workforce after raising a family. Do you know exactly what you need to do, but are unable to motivate yourself to do it?

Before I began writing this book, I found myself with no structure in my life. I had no accountability. I had no dreams. There was nothing I enjoyed, and on many levels, I didn't care if I lived or died. I believed the best years of my life were behind me and the trajectory of my life was on the decline. I had this unarticulated dream of writing a book, but I didn't know how to write it. All I had was my *Steven Typical Playlist*, a collection of my all-time favorite songs that soothed me when I didn't know I needed soothing, that kept me company when I didn't realize I was alone, that centered me when I didn't know I was askew. These songs, these friends of mine, were as dependable as death and gravity and taxes.

This book tells the story of a guy who actually does the things he suggests you do to change your life. He changed his life and so can you.

This book is about me pursuing my dream of being a published author and reclaiming the athletic, in-shape body I had for most of my adult life. It's also about building the support network to help me do it. I discuss the techniques I employed, the things I stopped doing, the new thoughts I inserted into my waking consciousness, and the new behaviors I forced myself to adopt. Having something to look forward to, even if it never happens, is HUGE, and is the gist of *Man's Search for Meaning* by Victor Frankl. In one of the twentieth century's most influential books in the field of psychology, Frankl proposes that the will to find meaning in life is the primordial, most driving force in humans. Writing this book can be seen as my will to find meaning.

Forty-five is the New Twenty-five teaches you how to make the things you dream about happen. If you are reading this book, written by this forty-five-year-old no one, you will likely see some of yourself in me, and that in some way or another you have struggled with the same things in which I have struggled.

One day recently, I came across a blog post by a guy named Nick Chiles. He writes, "I know that sometimes the most important thing I can do to spark my daughters' ambition is to simply tell them that they are capable."[1] Chiles' blog post recounts the journey of Phillis Wheatley, a slave who was eventually freed. In the 1770s, the family that owned Wheatley taught her to read and write English. She never let her origins or her past experiences constrain what she could become; Wheatley went on to become the first published African-American, female poet.

Jordin Sparks, a former "American Idol" winner, shares the same story Chiles references. "When I hear Wheatley's story and all she was able to accomplish during slavery, I am completely inspired. She was unaware that someone like herself was not supposed to read, let alone write a book. Her vision for her life was limitless and full of possibilities. Nothing stopped her from telling her story."

---

[1] Nick Chiles. MyBrownBaby blog, July 18, 2013. http://mybrownbaby.com/2013/07/the-kinsey-collection-jordin-sparks-introduces-black-girls-to-the-fierce-courage-of-phillis-wheatley/

I, too, am inspired by the story of Phillis Wheatley. Despite all of the falsely-constructed "differences" that supposedly exist between you and me, we are, in fact, not that different: this is something *I know to be true*. We are all the embodiment of an illiterate, enslaved Phillis Wheatley in one way or another. My struggles are your struggles, and your struggles are my struggles. The techniques that have worked for me to overcome the challenges I have faced *will* work for you. You just have to do them. You can't lie in bed ignoring the silent, inaudible reminders to behave differently that travel into your consciousness from a probable you that exists only in your dreams.

I have realized the simplest choices, the smallest actions—to go and start the shower, to make my bed, to put on an upbeat playlist, to water my plants, to fold my clothes, to put one foot in front of the other, to write down the things I dream about—are choices we make to live or not. "I Want To Live!" Susan Hayward, playing a woman convicted of murder and facing execution, proclaimed in the classic film noir named for her character's well-known line.

And I, too, want to live.

Steven stops writing his Introduction and gets up from the sofa in his TV room, walks over to the Lenovo touchscreen he uses to manage his iTunes, and selects "Stronger" by Kelly Clarkson. What doesn't kill us makes us...makes us what we are today.

SECTION 1
Starting My Book

You don't have to be great to start. You just have to start to be great.

—Zig Zigler

Chapter 1
Lost

In ABC's television series, *Lost,* one of the show's main plots pits the characters of Jack Shephard and John Locke against one another. Shephard, a medical doctor, represents rational skepticism. Locke, a wheelchair-bound "everyman," has his ability to walk restored after Oceanic Flight 815 crash lands onto the mysterious island. Locke represents an informed, blind faith of sorts and believes the island they are stranded on has some sort of mystical purpose for him and for all of the survivors of Oceanic Flight 815.

Rational skepticism and faith battle throughout the series. The rational skeptic would say a forty-five-year-old no one, who has not taken the steps to write regularly and/or to blog, cannot become an influential thought leader and published author. A more faith-based individual knows that anything is possible. The ideas inside this book will challenge the rational skeptics within us. They will challenge the voices we have in our heads that tell us we can't do something, and they are based on the non-physical laws of the universe that determine what we become. These laws should strengthen our blind faith to achieve our dreams, provided we are willing to write them down, and move toward them methodically and consistently.

The Livescribe® pen records all conversations during business meetings. The technology allows you to return to the dialogue at a later date. It "records everything you write, hear or say and allows you to replay your meetings simply by tapping on your notes." Steven does not use his pen for this, however. *I can barely sit through most meetings the first time. Why would I return to them?* Steven thinks to himself. Instead, he uses his pen to learn to be a better writer. It's like seeing a movie more than once. Like the countless times he has watched *Fried Green Tomatoes, The Way We Were,* or *It's a*

Wonderful Life. On subsequent viewings, you see, hear, and notice things you didn't the first time.

The pen is the same. You get to pay attention to the layers beneath the surface of the main plot.

Writing room at home
Sunday, September 30, 2012, 1:06 p.m.

Writing your own book and reading a book someone else has written is the difference between hosting a party and attending someone else's party. Hosting a party is lots of hard work, lots of planning and preparation, lots of logistics and communication. Attending a party is passive, while hosting a party is active.

Steven can't exactly describe the last five to eight years of his life as a party. No. It was probably much closer to a life of quiet desperation. In hindsight, without his *Steven Typical Playlist*, it was most definitely a life of quiet desperation. His was an existence camouflaged by the veneers we all use to cover the essence of who we are: a successful career, money, material things, close "friends," an enviable social life.

A while ago, I became obsessed with J.J. Abrams, the executive producer of Lost. *I found myself speed-watching six seasons of* Lost *on Netflix, determined to get to the end of the series so I could begin writing my book again. Every hour I sat engrossed in this television series, wondering what was going to happen next, I realized I was attending J.J. Abrams' party. I was distracting myself from the quiet desperation, transporting myself into someone else's world.*

In fact, research shows most Americans are as obsessed with watching television as Steven was watching *Lost*. Americans spend anywhere from twenty-eight to thirty-four hours per week watching television.[2]

Steven wonders how many others watch television to distract themselves from lives of quiet desperation. *I am finally ready to realize the J.J. Abrams inside of me*, Steven declares to himself. *I can host my own party. I can create my own world others will get lost in, rather than getting lost in someone else's world. First, I need to turn the TV off!* Steven thinks.

 A live version of Adele's "Make You Feel My Love" begins. Next is "Because of You" by Kelly Clarkson. Steven stares at the ceiling as Kelly sings, "My heart can't possibly break when it wasn't even whole to start with."

I want to write about the things I liked about the television show, Lost, *and the eighteen-minute TEDtalk I watched J.J. Abrams deliver on YouTube. In his TEDtalk, J.J. Abrams talked about the concept of a "mystery box," and the idea that mystery can be more important than knowledge. "The mystery box represents infinite possibility; it represents hope; it represents potential," J.J. explained. In the show, the writers would introduce the audience to a situation, a thing, a person (the black rock, Danielle, Juliet), and the reader or the audience is drawn in and wants to know more about the mystery. What is the black rock? Who is Danielle? Who is Juliet?*

Steven's mind wanders to two characters in his life and their mysteries. Who is Michele? Will my best friend be able to re-enter the workforce after raising her children? Can she prove her naysayers

---

[2]Hinckley, David. "Americans spend 34 hours a week watching TV, according to Nielsen numbers." New York Daily News, September 19, 2012. http://www.nydailynews.com/

wrong? Or have her naysayers always been right about her? Can someone really start a new career at forty-five-years-old? Is age just a number?

And he thinks of himself: Who is Steven? Can he overcome his struggles with discipline and depression? Is he delusional to think he can achieve his dreams at forty-five years old? Can he do the things he knows he needs to do to look and feel like he did when he was twenty-five? Will Steven always be just a frustrated dreamer?

One of the things done particularly well in Lost *was the portrayal of the duality that existed in its main characters. Is Shephard good because he seeks to save everyone, when in so many ways it is he who needs to be saved? Is Locke crazy? A desperate, lonely man running from the idea that he is just an ordinary man, determined to stay on the island where he can live under the delusion that he is special?*

Is this book my island, a milieu, where I am as delusional as John Locke? Is the real me some shackled, middle-aged no one who is invisible to the world-at-large around him? As I write this future for myself, is it just that, a *written* future? A me that exists only on these pages? Or, are the things I write about capable of impacting the me who is not in this book, a 45-year-old instructional designer who has failed repeatedly to write a cohesive, interesting, gripping work of nonfiction? On my island, can anyone be whatever he wants to be, the antithesis of everything he ever was?

People are not their résumés: They are more than the jobs they have held and not limited by the work experience they have already accrued. They have the option to create their own reality, as I am doing inside and outside of this book.

Lost seems to be ultimately about redemption and love. About the multidimensional, magical, transcendent qualities one can tap into by loving another human being wholly and completely.

Steven thinks of Michele again. *Does she have to find the strength within herself to rise above her circumstances? Perhaps she can piggyback on my strength until she develops the muscles she needs to stand on her own. Is love a force powerful enough to transcend time, circumstance, geography, language, intention, motivation, choice, and even fate itself? Or is fate just that, fate? Whatever will happen, will happen?*

***

Steven takes out his iPhone and sends a text.

> I AM SO EXCITED!!

Steven intentionally uses all caps in his text message to Michele because he truly is genuinely excited. *Michele isn't technologically-savvy enough to think, 'Why is Steven screaming at me?'* Steven chuckles to himself, full of that snarky attitude everyone loves about him. *I can't wait to tell Michele I have started my book again.*

Yet again, he is convinced his lifelong dream is about to come true, challenging his fate that he would never be more than "just a frustrated dreamer." When Steven was on his quest to discover the meaning of life in his mid- to late twenties, he was convinced he would always have all of these grandiose dreams, but never be able to achieve them in reality. He had accepted that the magical moments he would experience in this life would come when he was transported out of this world into the world of his imagination. In his twenties, he was convinced he would never, ever be more than a frustrated dreamer.

> What are you so excited about?
> Give me a call in a little bit after
> the kids have gone to bed.

Michele DiFranco (her maiden name, not her married name), has been Steven Sharp's best friend since they were five years old in Bloomfield, New Jersey. They went to grammar school, junior high, and high school together.

Michele's family is Steven's second family, and her mother is like a mother to him. Her family is the epitome of a New Jersey Italian-American family: loud, big Sunday family dinners, amazing dry meatballs. They still place a huge piece of plywood on their dining room table with a brightly-colored tablecloth over it so more people can squeeze around the table for holidays and family dinners. Steven, with his light brown hair and WASP heritage, always savored these big family dinners on Sundays at the DiFranco's. He'd sit at the table as if he belonged with Michele and her extended family.

She will always be DiFranco to me, he mused as he imagines what Michele's mother, Anna, must have sounded like with her impossibly-thick, complete New Jersey-Italian accent when she announced at the dinner table one evening, "Michelllle, Stayven is gonna' be gaaay, ya know?"

Glad I wasn't there for that one, Steven thinks to himself.

To this day, Steven loves to make Michele imitate her mother's voice, not that he exactly has to twist her arm. When they are on the phone together and Michele is upset about the topic du jour, Steven will interrupt Michele and ask her, "What would Anna say?"

Michele will immediately switch voices to sound like her mother. "Djayyysus Chrissssst, Michelllle ...that SonofaBetcch. I don't know why you put up with it, Michelllle?"

Next thing you know Steven is cracking up and usually Michele too, depending on how upset she is at the time.

I STARTED WRITING MY BOOK AGAIN!! I am very proud of you for getting your resume together and fixing your printer by yourself. Have a great evening and good night!!

Thank you Steven! Your kind supportive words are very nice to hear:) And that is awesome about your book!! I can't wait to hear more about it.

He's writing his book again? I wonder what it's about this time... Michele thinks as she types a supportive response.

A couple of days later, Steven is pulling a handful of his fat away from his abdomen while taking a side profile selfie of his huge gut when he receives a text message from Michele.

Hi steven... I'm really upset right now n I need to talk to you about something

Steven switches from his photos app so he can reply to Michele's text.

OK, I'll call in a sec.

OK

> OK. I am going to call you from Skype.

> K

> Having to upgrade software it'll take a second or two. Hold tight:-)

> Hope it doesn't take as long as my printer driver update... good luck!

Logitech® Wireless Headsets and calling from Skype

"Michele? Hey it's me! What's up?" Steven reaches under his kitchen sink and grabs the can of stainless steel cleaner.

"I just took the kids by myself to IHOP because it's 'kids-eat-free-night' and they always have a character there to entertain them."

"What do you mean 'a character?'" Steven hoses down his refrigerator with a thick coat of the milky white, creamy cleaner.

"Well, they are not real characters because that would cost too much money, so tonight they had *Mouse Girl*, but it is really Minnie Mouse...Last week they had *The Sponge Guy*, but it was really Sponge Bob."

Steven bursts out in hysterical laughter as he grabs a thick wad of paper towels. "Wait a minute; they have fake Disney characters to lure families with kids? Does it work?"

"Apparently. We were there," Michele's laugh starts with a giggle and erupts into a few seconds of release. *I wish Michele had a webcam so I could see her laughing.* "So anyway...the kids are all wild, and I have to get them ready for bed soon."

"So what are you so upset about?" Steven starts polishing the top right corner of his side-by-side KitchenAid, moving his right arm in a circular motion.

"I don't know if you remember that awhile back I applied for these grants that would allow me to go back and complete some courses I need for my education specialist degree?"

"Yes. Of course I remember."

"Well I got put on this waiting list and every few weeks I would call and talk to my counselor to see if my name came up to receive the grant. The counselor would always tell me that I could look up the status of my application online, but I could never figure out how to do it."

As he is getting down on his knees to polish the bottom right side of the refrigerator, Steven braces himself against the doors, staring through them, willing this story to have a different ending than all of Michele's other stories.

"Every time I called, I was told that there were tons of applicants and not that many grants available each quarter. So...of course everyone in my negative, non-supportive family thought I was nuts for calling each month, and they wanted me to give it up, and they wouldn't even listen to me if I tried to talk about it. But I was hopeful, because they pay for your whole schooling and you don't have to pay it back."

"How long did you stay on the waiting list?" Steven kneels motionlessly in front of his refrigerator.

"Three years."

Nope. This story is going to end like all the other ones. There is a moment of audible silence before they erupt into uncontrollable laughter, maybe tinged with a little bit of nervousness. *Why did she put all of her eggs in this one basket?*

"So of course all of the naysayers in my family were proven right."

"When was the last time you called?" He stands up, moving to the left side.

"I called a couple of weeks ago and my counselor told me the list expired and my name was no longer on the list, and I would have to reapply...So of course I am going to reapply; a part of me feels like I'm going to go through the same cycle again, and it's going to be another three years wasted and I'm going to be dropped off the waiting list and still be exactly where I am now. The worst part about it is...if this happens, all of the naysayers will be right. It just reminds me of when I was a little girl. I always had all of these ideas and never had ANY support from any one in my family."

Michele changes her naturally funny, sweet tone and affects a biting, derogatory, belittling tone, most likely imitating her father this time, "'Whattaya' want to do that for, Michele? That's so stupid. Don't even go there Michele, you'll make a fool out of yourself.'" Michele switches back to her natural tone. "I decided to apply again...I have to go down for a meeting and since Ava is not in school yet, I needed someone to watch the kids, so I asked Patrick if he could watch the kids," Michele switches tones again, imitating her husband, Patrick, this time. "'You don't think you're doing that, do ya?' Patrick said to me with this real exasperated, nasty tone in his voice. So then I called

Sharon and asked her if she could watch Ava so I could go in and apply." Sharon is Michele's oldest sister.

"Sharon said, 'You're crazy, Michele. You're forty-five years old. You should be thinking about retiring, not going back to school.' Steven, I just sat there dumbfounded. She told me she and her husband are thinking of buying a place in Florida soon and moving. As I listened to Sharon and her thoughts of retiring at forty-seven, I thought that I could work for another twenty-five years. I don't know what upset me more: the way she talked...talks to me, or that she believes her life is on the downhill. I just wish for once I could have my family's full support; that they would think I am smart, rather than the joke of the family."

"Michele, you have to earn their support. Forty-five is the new twenty-five, ya know. Don't listen to your fucking family."

"What did you say?"

"Don't listen to your fucking family?"

Michele laughs out loud. "No not that. The thing about forty-five."

"Forty-five is the new twenty-five...I'll help you prove the naysayers wrong!"

"You really think I can prove the naysayers wrong?"

"Yes, I really do."

"Thanks, Steven! You always make me feel better."

As he and Michele say their goodbyes, Steven notices the shadow of his silhouette as he admires his perfectly polished refrigerator. He removes his headset somewhat robotically as he moves over to the dishwasher.

Chapter 2
Forty-five is the New Twenty-five?

Forty-five is the new twenty-five? Steven ponders this play on the commonly-used "_____ is the new black" expression. *What does that mean?* Steven thinks, and immediately an answer forms in his mind. *I don't know, but it would be a great title for a book.*

At twenty-five, most people are just starting their careers. They believe their whole lives are still ahead of them, that they can do anything they set their minds to do, like Phillis Wheatley did[3]. She didn't know she wasn't supposed to learn how to read. She put her mind to it and she did it. At forty-five, Michele is trying to start her career after raising three children. Steven is trying to become a published author. *Can we put our minds to it and do it? Do other people struggle with this?*

Hmmmmmm, Steven thinks. *Maybe there is a lost generation of people trapped in unfulfilling careers, with unrealized, fading dreams, who believe their lives have passed them by. Maybe there are a bunch of Stevens out there who are happy in their careers, but have dreams they don't dare themselves to dream anymore.*

In fact there are. Recent studies show that anywhere from 70-80 percent of workers are not engaged in the work they perform, and therefore, not happy in their career. So why do people stay? People stay because they need the paycheck: they have children and families to support, student loans to pay off, and retirement to save for. In most cases, people construct a life based on what they can "afford" at their current income levels. What an individual makes determines where he lives, what he drives, if he can afford to eat out or take a vacation, and whether he shops in discount or retail stores. How we

---

[3] Nick Chiles. MyBrownBaby blog, July 18, 2013. http://mybrownbaby.com/2013/07/the-kinsey-collection-jordin-sparks-introduces-black-girls-to-the-fierce-courage-of-phillis-wheatley/

spend money becomes entrenched in who we are, making it difficult to change.

People also stay in unfulfilling careers because the experience and skills they have obtained have value. If we have invested years of our lives earning a doctorate degree, why would we abandon the security and prestige of a $95,000 per year job as a clinical psychologist to accept an entry-level position as a corporate recruiter, even though that's what we want to do? We invest years of our lives and spend tens or hundreds of thousands of dollars earning advanced degrees. Our educations, the job skills and experience we gain as we support ourselves—coupled with how we spend and budget money—shackles us to unfulfilling, unrewarding careers. We stay in unsatisfactory careers because we don't know how to leave, we know leaving would be hard and we are scared.

People in their sixties, seventies, and eighties generally worked in one job or industry for their entire careers and then retired; however, today's generations are different. It is not uncommon to have three, four, or more careers in one's working life. According to Carl Bialik in the September 2, 2010, *Wall Street Journal* article "Seven Careers in a Lifetime? Think Twice, Researchers Say," "...the average U.S. worker will have many careers—seven is the most widely cited number—in his or her lifetime."

Steven ponders the title of his book some more. What if forty-five could really be the new twenty-five? That people's futures are not determined by the jobs they have had in the past, that people are not their résumés. That who they can become is not determined by the things they have already accomplished, but instead by the things they hope to accomplish.

What are the practical, doable things people can do to change jobs? What obstacles must they overcome? How can they convince a potential employer to give them a chance when they no longer have youth on their side?

Steven takes a break and peruses Facebook® for a few moments. He comes across a post from Stephanie Thomson who worked for Steven as an instructional design intern over the summer:

Stephanie Thomson

There is a story in the book of Luke where Jesus talks about giving a banquet. He says that when you give a banquet, do not invite your friends, brothers or sisters, relatives, or rich neighbors, for they can all pay you back. But invite the poor, the crippled, the lame, the blind, for none of them can give you anything in return. Bless them, for they cannot bless you back.

Steven stares at the screen, thinking about this parable from the Bible and his friend Stephanie. If one were to scroll through Stephanie's Facebook timeline, you would see a faith-based senior at Auburn University, pictures of her family and lots of friends getting married.

Dan Chase stops at Steven's desk, interrupting his train of thought.

"How do you feel after our run?" asks Dan.

It takes Steven a moment to process what Dan has asked him. "Out of shape. Sore. Mad at myself for getting so out of shape," Steven responds honestly, grimacing slightly.

"Just take it slowly, Steven. Let's go get some coffee," Dan suggests. "Stick with it. It'll get easier."

Dan Chase works with Steven in the training center of their company, and is in top-notch shape. On Twitter he describes himself as a "Princess Syndrome Enabler" and "Gentleman Raiser." These labels reference his two beautiful children he has with his wife Kristen. They went running one day, and Steven enrolled Dan in being his workout partner. Steven will frequently joke that Dan burns more calories every day convincing him to get to the gym than they actually burn while working out!

Steven and Dan walk over to Human Resources to get their coffees, and they overhear Amelia O'Connor talking about a period in her life when she had an existential epiphany. Amelia is a brunette with bright expressive eyes, a genuine smile, and a spontaneous immediacy to her laugh.

Steven can't believe what he is hearing: Amelia's existential epiphany is related to changing careers, months shy of a Ph.D. in clinical psychology. What are the chances that Amelia would be talking about this at the coffee machine as Steven and Dan approached?

The universe is supporting this book I am writing, Steven thinks. *I'll have to follow up with her.*

Chapter 3
Strengths/Likes and Weaknesses/Dislikes

Amelia O'Connor Interview
Wednesday, May 11, 2013, 2:00 p.m.

Steven slowly and neatly scrawls "Amelia O'Connor Interview," across
the top of the page as he waits for Amelia to arrive for his inaugural
book interview. There is deliberateness to the cadence of his
handwriting.

She arrives and relaxes in the chair across from Steven. Steven begins
the interview.

"So, I have put out to the universe that I am writing this book and you
appeared out of nowhere sharing this story about your existential
epiphany and career change! I can't wait to hear more…When we
were in the break room that day, you said you created this diagram of
things that you liked or enjoyed doing and things that you didn't like
or didn't enjoy doing. Can you tell me more about this process you
followed?"

"Sure! I made a couple of columns kind of like this," Amelia draws a T
diagram on a piece of paper for Steven. "On the right I put a
combination of strengths as well as likes, and on the left I put
weaknesses and dislikes."

"Why did you choose to write down your likes, dislikes, strengths, and
weaknesses?"

"I knew from my training as a cognitive-behavioral therapist…to truly
make a change, I needed to be an active participant in driving the

process...I also wanted to be able to make a clear distinction between what I knew about myself at that point in my life."

Amelia's reasoning follows a circuitous path when attempting to explain most things, and this time is no different. "My father always said to me when I was little, you need to find something you love and are passionate about and figure out how to make money doing it. So this was my attempt to try and figure out what it was I liked, what I was passionate about, and could make money doing."

"Did you read this technique in a magazine or talk to a career counselor, or did you make it up?"

"I made it up. It was based on my father's advice. I started with personality stuff, like I like working with people; I like solving problems; I like improving things; I like pleasing others; I like making other people happy. I hadn't really been part of the corporate world so I didn't really know what I was writing down; it was like stream of consciousness."

"OK, so since you were not familiar with corporate America jargon, how did you come up with the buzz words?"

"I reached out to a lot of the professional people I knew..."

"They would read your list and say, 'that is process improvement,' 'that is team building,' et cetera?"

"YES. I needed others to help me with the buzz words and industry-specific terminology."

"So, all you did was get in touch with what you liked?"

"Yup. That's about it." A wide, tall grin spreads across her face.

"OK. What were your weaknesses and dislikes? Do you remember?"

"Ummm. I didn't like red tape; I didn't like bureaucracy. I didn't like...you know, I really can't remember. I do remember at the time it was a really long list." Amelia chuckles loudly and her soft brown eyes glow brightly.

Steven leans forward and interrupts her. "That is an excellent sign! This process you took yourself through has allowed you to move through your once-perceived weaknesses and dislikes."

"Yes. I would agree with that."

"This is a really strong endorsement of the process you followed. OK...I interrupted you before when you said you got people to help you with the buzzwords—what was that process like?"

"I actually handed the piece of paper over to my friends and my family members and asked them to be honest with me about the qualities on the list."

"But you were lucky enough to come from a very professional family anyway?"

"Yes. I was."

"And your friends are Ph.D.s, college graduates, professionals. A lot of people who are going to be reading this book are not going to have the same network as you, so I will have to come up with some ideas for them."

"True. But I think you can ask anyone. Ask people at church, anyone in your network of people you interact with."

"I don't know if I agree with you...I don't know that anyone would know someone that could label something 'process improvement.'"

"That's true." Amelia somewhat reluctantly agrees with him.

"But that's beside the point." Steven redirects the conversation. "So you said there were three things you asked them to do?"

"I asked them to add to the list on both sides—strengths/likes and weaknesses/dislikes—based on what they knew about my personality...And there were times when people would insist I put something on the strengths side and I had to disagree. If I didn't enjoy it and it was a strength, I didn't want it on that side of the list.

"Next, I asked them to help me with the tags, the buzz words, the catch phrases. We translated the list of my strengths and what I enjoyed into industry-specific terminology, business competencies, and job skills."

Steven holds up a hand for Amelia to stop. "That's very clear. I had to update my résumé recently, and since I had never invested a lot of time or energy into my résumé I hired a professional to help me with the buzz words. I was very pleased with the results. We got it done in two days, and it cost $500."

"WOW! That's a lot of money."

"Yes, it is, but I was interviewing for a director's position and I didn't want my résumé to be all ghetto."

"You're hilarious...and slightly inappropriate," Amelia needles Steven, putting on her Human Resources hat for a moment. "The last thing I did after I felt like I had an exhaustive list of my strengths, was ask them what profession I should go into, like what does this translate into?"

"And, at the time you did this, you had no idea about the Human Resources profession?"

"No, I really didn't. It was resounding I should go into Human Resources...So I went to Monster® and posted a résumé with no experience seeking an entry-level corporate recruiter position."

"Do you think it was your advanced degrees that got you an interview with no experience?"

"It may have been that, but I was also really humble and was willing to take an entry-level role. It wasn't about salary for me. I recognized where I was in my career, and I recognized that in order to make a transition I needed to be realistic. Between the online profile you complete and my résumé, I was clear I was looking for an entry-level position for an employer that was willing to train me, and I expected an entry-level salary."

"Got it. Got it," Steven says, nodding his head as he concludes the interview with Amelia.

As Steven finishes transcribing this part of Amelia's interview, he contemplates the career transition process Amelia led herself through. It was intentional; it was thorough; it was time-consuming; it was simple. She didn't do it alone. She leveraged her network including her friends, her extended family, and her classmates— individuals she respected. She was realistic; she knew she'd have an entry-level salary and wouldn't have a corner office any time soon. Amelia knew the first couple of years would require certain concessions, and she was more than willing to make them.

Amelia never shared the specifics of her existential epiphany, the events that caused her to leave her Ph.D. program in the first place.

He pauses for a moment to reflect upon how much he has accomplished in the five months since he conducted this interview with Amelia. He thinks about the goals he has set for himself and the techniques he has employed to achieve them. As he sits alone in his writing room, he contemplates the friendship he and Amelia have formed and how much he enjoys having her in his life. He also considers how incredibly bright she is: Amelia understands you can't merely "know" what your strengths are and what you enjoy; *she realizes you must write them down to make them real.*

Chapter 4
Negotiate an Unpaid Internship

Amelia O'Connor Interview (continued)
Wednesday, May 11, 2013, 2:00 p.m.

"There is one other thing that I think is incredibly relevant and a huge contributor to my success in changing careers. I reached out to a colleague and negotiated a three-month, unpaid internship for myself to get the corporate experience I needed to be more marketable," Amelia continues. "Interestingly, the internship I secured for myself ended up paying $20 per hour. So, not only did I get the experience I so desperately needed, I received a livable wage."

"That is great advice," Steven agrees. "I used to run a small business. I think people changing careers have a tremendous opportunity selling themselves as free labor to an entrepreneurial company to gain the experience they need. If the intern works extremely hard and consistently exceeds expectations, most business owners would find a way to compensate the intern."

"OK…" Steven moves on. "Back to you. So from when you first started the process to change careers until you landed this job where you work now, how long did the process take?"

"About three years…Generally speaking, I think that is a pretty reasonable timeframe. I mean you need the foundational experience to get you to the next level."

"So the process you led yourself through landed you an entry-level job as a corporate recruiter." Steven pauses as he regroups to switch gears. "Today, in your role as a recruiter, do you always look for certain things, regardless of the probable age of the candidate?"

"I do. Depending on what the job is…There are a number of things that I look at. Certainly if I am looking at a candidate who is super strong and super seasoned and they are applying directly for more of a mid-career or entry-level role, I have questions as to why this person is willing to take this drop back. This is something that needs to be addressed somewhere: in the online application, on the résumé, or during initial screening."

Amelia is lost in the world of what she has learned about corporate recruiting. She pauses, remembering.

Amelia continues, "If this question isn't addressed, the manager of the position will wonder if the candidate is going to jump ship in six months if a better opportunity comes along…."

"On the flip side," suggests Steven, "it may be a new mom who has been in a high-level position in the past, but her focus now is on her family. The position she is applying for might allow her to leave exactly at 5:30 or 6:00 p.m. every day and never have to bring her laptop home with her."

"Exactly. And she will be the most dedicated employee for the next five to ten years. This stuff is not always communicated in the résumé, but it absolutely needs to be. Your experience needs to match the position you are applying for, and if doesn't, you need to address this concern head on, somewhere."

"So if someone goes in with realistic expectations—I'm talking about my book now—and they are forty, forty-two, or forty-five, they are going to be forty-three, forty-five, or forty-eight eventually anyway. Why not invest the time *now* to create a career that excites you? I would much prefer to spend three years creating a future life for myself I would look forward to living, than using those same three years doing nothing, unaware or pretending that dreading work is not a huge problem."

"I agree with you one hundred percent. I devised and followed a good process. I think when you come in with that level of maturity at that age, you are kind of fast-tracked. Part of this is my bias because I was actually a professor at several different universities, but my favorite students were always the ones who had been out in the world in real life and had worked and were trying to better themselves. These were the students that were always super responsible, receptive, and eager to learn. These were the ones that always did all of their work above and beyond. And…they were excited; they were *hungry*…When comparing the twenty-year-old college generation with people in their thirties, forties, and even fifties who return to school, I honestly believe because of differences in their work ethics, approaches, and levels of maturity the older generation is advantaged in the workplace."

"I think that brings us to a great stopping place, Amelia! Thank you so much for sharing all of this great information!"

A couple of months later, Steven designs a recruiting brochure for Amelia to thank her for being interviewed for his book. During the brochure's final editing meeting, Amelia identifies each change needed, and as Steven works to implement the changes, the conversation shifts to his book.

"Ya know, I am dying to know what ends up in the book," Amelia says über-dramatically.

"I think you will be happy with it." Steven fishes out the marked up manuscript and begins flipping through it. "Since I had to cut out so much of what you shared with me, I wanted to discuss something with you."

"Ummmmmm. Okaaaaayyyy," Amelia's face pales and her cheeks become flushed. "That makes me a little nervous."

"There is nothing to be nervous about. We had a really interesting interview. Two things clearly stand out for me when I go back and review the transcript."

"What are they?"

"I was struck by two main forces that influenced the choices you made: (1) forces outside of yourself, various externalities; and (2) your internal thought processes, logic, and critical thinking skills. For whatever reason, at this period in your life, these two sets of forces battled violently, and you became the unwitting and unknowing victim of these forces."

"Interesting…Wow…That's deep. I need to think about this some. What led you to this conclusion?" Her body is in the room, but her mind is in the post-graduate years of her life.

"Providing a good answer to that question could be its own book. The short answer is: I am writing a book; I one hundred percent believe the universe is laying all of these situations and events out in front of me, and it is my job to figure out what it all means. To go a little deeper…your character, your story, and what led you to your existential crisis is a microcosm of the career satisfaction levels of the entire United States' current workforce. You working on your Ph.D. program in clinical psychology when you wanted to be a fashion designer represents the estimated 70-80 percent of Americans who are unsatisfied and unfulfilled in their current jobs. Why were you on the wrong career path? What led you there? I am confident the factors that led Amelia O'Connor to her personal breaking point are some of the same factors responsible for the low levels of career satisfaction in this country."

"Wow. That's profoundly deep."

"Well...during the interview, you identify specific external forces that influenced and informed the decisions you made. These choices you made led you to the place where you were completely miserable in your career."

"That is true. I do remember sharing these things with you several times throughout the interview."

"Since it did not directly relate to helping someone change careers, I eliminated all of it. However, I found myself wanting to include certain details, but they would have made no sense without other details. It was either most of it, or none at all."

Amelia looks at Steven earnestly and thoughtfully. "I am not sure I understand what you are saying, if there is a question in there, and if you want a response?"

"I want you to think about something...You identified specific external forces that influenced the decisions you made back then...You may have even said you would have made different choices if you knew then what you know now."

"Yeah. I think I did say that."

"This book is about learning, growing, changing, evolving, and helping. I know my readers would benefit greatly if you would consider sharing some of the personal details of your existential epiphany that led you to a career in Human Resources...Just think about it. We can change your name if we need to. These personal stories will strengthen the book and help to make it the best it can be."

As Steven finishes basically pleading with Amelia to share her stories with his readers, he runs and grabs his phone and sends Michele a text.

Michele, I am finding out some great career stuff for you.

Really? Like what?

A simple, straightforward process anyone can follow to identify ur personal strengths and style preferences and align them with a rewarding profession that values the skills you already have

WOW! You're right. That does sound exciting. I would love to do something like that.

OK. You can test the technique and provide feedback before the book gets published.

Chapter 5
What's Going on with the 25-Year-Olds?

From: **Steven Sharp**
To: **Stephanie Thomson**
Subject: **Letter to Stephanie # 1**

Dear Stephanie,

The voice of Tori Amos fills my home at 5:22 a.m. on the day you are leaving to drive back to Auburn. The song's name is "Winter," and it has ended, much like your internship has. Now, "Goodbye Alice in Wonderland" by Jewel keeps my moist eyes and peaceful demeanor company as I write to you. The peace I understand: these two songs are a part of my *Steven Typical Playlist*, a collection of songs that have soothed my soul so many countless times since the invention of the iPod. When I am alone in my house and these songs serenade me; I am never alone. They are a mother's arms, her hugs of a frightened child who is not destined to have a family of his own.

I realize I haven't fully described the feeling of peace to you as an accomplished, published, *New York Times Bestselling* author would. Yes, I can refer to myself as a "*New York Times Bestselling*" author for lots of reasons - even though it is yet to happen. If Teresa Guidice of *The Real Housewives of New Jersey* has the audacity to describe herself as a *New York Times Bestselling* Author, certainly the prospect of me being able to accomplish this same feat is not out of the realm of possibility.

So, the other emotion, the moist eyes and quivering lips, pressed together tightly now. I miss your bright smile and eager thirst for knowledge and understanding; your joy emanates from the inside of you; it is not one that is artfully-constructed in some calculated way. For whatever reason, as people age they become less like you, less like me too, I guess. Or maybe they were never like us to begin with? That is another "song" for another day, as "Irvine" by Kelly Clarkson soothes me.

Let's look for ways we can be teachers of each other and students of each other in our post-work friendship.

Your friend,

Steven

About a month later, Steven receives an email response from Stephanie. The first line of Stephanie's email reassures him that she doesn't think he is bat-shit crazy, at least not yet anyway.

From: **Stephanie Thomson**
To: **Steven Sharp**
Subject: **RE: Letter to Stephanie # 1**

Steven,

Hi! Great email!!! Let me jump right in...

You mentioned many songs throughout your last letter. You revealed that your music is very dear to you. I feel the same way. As I write to you, I am listening to the song "Inside It All Feels the Same" by an instrumental band called Explosions in the Sky. For whatever reason, this band makes me feel even though there are no words to accompany the melodies. Yet, music does so much more than just make me feel; music has been my friend.

Music has been a comfort to me. It has helped to heal my once broken heart. And as you mentioned in your letter, it has been warm arms to hold me when everyone else's arms just felt cold. I enjoy hearing about the music that other people listen to because not only does that expose me to new artists, but it also gives me a small glimpse into another dimension of their personality. My opinion is that when you, Steven Sharp, include some of your favorite songs in your letters, it integrates a very vital part of your personality into the ideas of your book. Is that one of the reasons you chose to share some songs with me?

One of the things you asked me to do is to help you remember what it is like to be a college student. College has been a life-changing season for me because my past experiences have begun to fulfill their purpose in my life, turning me into the person that I am destined to become.

As Steven reads this part of Stephanie's email, he thinks about the quote his friend Bryan shared with him recently, "The best time to plant a tree is twenty years ago. The second-best time is now." Steven continues reading Stephanie's thoughtful email.

I tend to like to look at the big picture. Someday, just as the experiences I had in middle and high school have come together to make me who I am today, my college experiences will determine who I am to someday become. Therefore, I believe that now is the time to figure out who that person will be! I am determined not to waste this life.

Steven pauses for a moment and thinks to himself, *Oh! To be twenty-one years old again, determined not to waste the life we have been given and the potential we have.*

Rather than spending my nights drinking and waking up the next morning with no recollection of the night before, I choose to spend my time in other ways. I do things that inspire me. I choose to participate in things that expose me to the beauty of this life, despite all the darkness of our present world. Through these experiences, I have slowly begun to figure out my strengths. I believe that someday I am supposed to use those strengths to fulfill a greater purpose, though I'm not sure yet what that greater purpose is. We are gifted with minds that can think, hands that can do good and hearts that can love. Why wouldn't we want to be all that we can be and use every talent that we've been blessed with?

As I close this letter, the song "Look into the Air" by Explosions in the Sky comes to an end. I hope that everything is going well in your life and that your book writing is progressing!

Sincerely,

Stephanie

"...hands that can do good and hearts that can love." These words play over and over again in Steven's mind as he finishes reading Stephanie's email. *Hearts that can love...*

Steven stares at his computer screen wondering if he will ever have the courage to "stray from the sidewalk" and if he will always "play on the safe side" as the lyrics and melody of "Because of You" by Kelly Clarkson take over his brain.

Steven checks his Facebook account and receives an unexpected string of messages from his friend Bryan Hawn.

Bryan Hawn

Steven call me... I miss you

or text me LOL

Let's do something tonight and hang out like we used to. Miss you!!!!!!!!!! I can't wait to tell you about my new book, *The List: 360*. It's 128 pages, and I am really proud of it.

WTF? Bryan is only twenty-nine years old and he has written a book that is 128 pages, and I am forty-five and still haven't realized my dream of being a published author? I wonder what Bryan knows about accomplishing a lifelong goal that I don't?

Bryan Hawn has been Steven's friend since Bryan was nineteen years old. Bryan is one of the only kindred spirits Steven has found in the gay community. Bryan is incredibly positive and so full of life and love. He loves music, performing, and physical fitness. His latest energy is being spent establishing himself as a fitness guru. Bryan lives his life as if the best years of his life are still ahead of him.

Once Steven arrives to pick up Bryan, he sends him a text message.

> Hey! I'm here. Out front... not sure if I should be at the servant's entrance or not?

Bryan is staying in the guest house of his dad's mansion in historic Buckhead for a few days while he is in Atlanta. As Bryan opens the car door, they exchange greetings and start talking like it hasn't been months or even years since they have seen each other. "Hey Big Bry!"

"Hi Steven!" Bryan closes the door and fastens his seat belt.

"I can't wait to hear about your book. What's it called again?"

"*The List: 360.*"

"Great title. I love that you are referencing your first book's title, *The List*. Very smart, Bryan!" Steven compliments Bryan with this slightly patronizing, harmless tone he uses from time to time.

"Thank you, Steven."

"You know I am writing a book, too?"

"Yes, I saw that on Facebook! Steven, you have been writing that book since I met you, and I was nineteen," Bryan deadpans, and then cracks up, and they both start laughing.

"I know I have, but this time I think it is for real," Steven answers earnestly. It's hard not to believe Steven when he tells you something, even if it is that he's writing his book for real this time. "I have been thinking a lot about goals lately. All of our energy goes to surviving, we have little energy left for the things we want to do, ya know? I have finally written down my goal to be a published author. I think writing it down makes all the difference."

"Wow! That's powerful. I talk a lot about goals in my book, too."

"So when do I get an autographed copy of your book? Also, how did you write and publish a 128-page book so quickly?"

"I'll download a copy of the book now to your hard drive. That'll be your autographed copy," Bryan starts laughing again. "For two solid weeks I wrote from six in the morning until two in the morning. I did that every day until the book was completed."

"That is amazing! Congratulations, Bryan. You have to be a character in my book."

"I thought I *was* a character in your book," Bryan smirks and responds with a sarcastic tone in his voice.

Oh yeah. I did kind of tell Bryan he was a character in my book, but that was ten years ago…Of course I had been propositioning anyone with a pulse back then to be a character in my book.

The next day, Dan stops at Steven's desk on the way to the men's room.

"It's Wednesday; you're doing Jason's class with me, right?" Dan says to Steven with a slightly challenging tone in his voice.

"Don't I always do Jason's class with you on Wednesdays?"

"No, actually ya don't."

"Well I am today! Come get me at 12:45 p.m."

"What? No meetings to attend? Or forgotten sneakers? And you have your workout clothes?"

"Nope. I'm all in." *At least for today I am.*

Chapter 6
Perfection Exists Within Your Imperfections

Steven stays in bed until after 7:00 a.m. As he lies there, he tries to coax himself out of bed and is unable to. *You need to get out of bed when you wake up; not lay there like you have done so many times in the past.* Steven rolls over and burrows back under the covers.

Even the smallest, tiniest steps are decisions we make to live or die. And, I want to live! Lying in bed when we are awake is choosing to die. On top of choosing to die by being unable to extract himself from bed, he sees Julie has texted him.

> Hey SS! Its Julie. How's the food journal going?

Julie Jones is the personal trainer he recently hired to help him with discipline and getting back in shape.

It's not.

> Oh, It's going...

Steven lays there like a mummy, unable to extract himself from the bed. *Focus on the things you want for yourself, Steven:*

1. I want to be a bestselling author.

2. I want to lead a lunch and learn program to build the Microsoft Office skills and raise productivity of the corporate employees where I work.

3. I want to be famous.

Well, ya can't be famous lying in bed, too lazy to get up. So get the eff up…Baby steps, Steven. Small steps will walk you out of the misery of the life you are living into the life you have always dreamed of living. When you are depressed and can't motivate yourself to do anything, if you can just force yourself to start moving, doing anything—walking to water the parched plants on your balcony, circling your bed to make it, folding a load of clothes—you give yourself a fighting chance against the depression. An object in motion stays in motion.

Steven finally gets up. By now, Michele has texted him, too.

> I haven't heard from you in a while. Are you OK?

Steven dumps a huge amount of Coffee-mate® in a mug of left-over coffee and sticks it in the microwave to warm, since he can't for the life of him tell the difference between day-old coffee and a "fresh" pot…like they put on in the movies when a neighbor stops over to talk to you about something important. He walks back to the bedroom and starts making the bed. Steven's bed has a top sheet, a blanket, a comforter, and six pillows. He straightens the top sheet on one side and walks to the other side and finishes smoothing the top sheet. He then pulls the blanket up and matches it to the top of the top sheet exactly. He walks around the bed again and matches the blanket to the top of the top sheet on the other side of the bed.

I don't want to read a book about a fucking guy making his fucking bed. Steven's Naysayer's voice fills his head. *It's about intentional behavior and shows attention to detail,* Steven counters his Naysayer as he continues his bed-making morning ritual, folding his white fluffy down comforter in half, making sure the top sheet and blanket are exposed. He has to take at least a thousand more steps to make his bed the way he likes it, walking from side to side of his queen-sized bed. On the mornings he struggles, making his bed is a long, protracted process that takes him several minutes or more. It is one of the techniques he uses to get his day started and combat whatever makes him not want to get out of bed. He has trained himself to immediately start moving to make his bed once he is no longer in it.

Steven walks over to his computer and starts "Stronger" by Kelly Clarkson.

Walk to the dryer and heat the load of colored clothes you washed last night so you can fold them as you drink your coffee. As Steven begins folding his clothes, he remembers he must bring his lunch and workout clothes to work every day. Steven has realized in getting from where he is to where he is going—wherever that may be—is as simple as moving. *Just move*, Steven soothes himself. *Just move.*

If you are moving in the wrong direction, the "timeless-you" (your soul, your spirit) will tell you to change your course. For your part, you just have to move and listen to that internal voice. He finishes the laundry, gets dressed, and heads out for a second cup at Dancing Goats Coffee Bar in Ponce City Market in Atlanta's Old Fourth Ward.

Yes, I am OK. Struggling with motivation as usual.

I hear ya. I can't motivate myself to do anything either.

While in Dancing Goats, he receives a phone call from Michele and steps outside to take the call. "You sound down."

"I feel like such a failure, Steven. I haven't done anything with my life. I am forty-five years old and I haven't accomplished anything, and now I fear I never will."

Steven grows quiet as he begins to pace around the screened-in porch outside the coffee bar. Inside of Michele is an intensity that burns, perhaps even more intensely than what burns inside of him. "Michele, I don't think it is too late for you. Lots of people change careers in their forties. Or, in your case, start their careers after raising children. I can help you get a plan together to re-enter the workforce."

"You would do that for me?"

"Yes, I would do that for you. You need to start with the list of your likes and dislikes, strengths and weaknesses," referencing the plan Amelia suggested.

"OK. I'll work on it. I promise."

Three weeks later

Did I really have the confidence and the stupidity to post to Facebook on April 1 of all days (I guess the joke is truly on me):

Steven Sharp

Day two of Steven's recommitment to getting in shape like he used to be!!! Wish me luck people!! Send encouragement my way!!!

Let's see...a total of eight exclamation points for twenty-two words. That is greater than one exclamation point for every three words. It's obvious to me that writing a book to help someone re-enter the workforce after a prolonged absence, change careers, and/or get in shape is going to take more than a single Facebook post with eight effing exclamation points.

Steven's more enlightened, internal voice materializes: *There is no judgment here, Steven. You are perfect as you are and exactly where you need to be. Don't beat yourself up; this book already exists...you ask yourself what was missing from the plan. You've started; now listen for the answer on what's next. You add what is missing and you continue moving forward to where you want to be. You ask for help if you need it.*

What was missing from my exercise plan? Immediately the answer materializes in his psyche from the timeless part of himself:

1. You need specific times of the day.

2. You need easy access to the schedule—out of sight equals out of mind.

3. You need to design a tracking sheet that tracks your daily activities that either moves you closer to the body you had at twenty-five or further away from it.

Steven reads the next entry in his notebook, remembering the frustration he felt and how he addressed it when he was composing this passage.

What was the last thing I wrote for this effing book I don't know how to write?

Is that true? as Byron Katie would say. (As a side note, Byron Katie's career as an author began when she had an epiphany at forty-four years old.)

No, actually it isn't true. I know exactly how to write this book. The universal consciousness, the cells that form my identity today, at one time comprised the identity of someone who knew exactly how to write this book. And my conscious awareness will one day inhabit a future Steven Sharp who knows exactly how to write this book. Therefore, I know right now exactly how to write this book.

I ALREADY KNOW.

June 26, 2012, 5:19 a.m.
Logitech® Wireless Headsets

Steven dictates with his headset in an attempt to convey his *taedium vitae,* as he starts to match up the colored socks that never got folded from the last load of colors he did. As he reaches his hand into a sock, he hears his mother's voice in his head: *Steven, please turn your socks right side out before you put them into the dirty clothes.* Steven finds it hard to believe his mother has been dead for over twelve years, and he contemplates what it must have been like for his mother: working full time, raising three sons, and always making sure they had perfectly-matched socks, turned right-side out.

No one wants to read a book about you rearranging your fucking sock drawer, Steven's Naysayer's voice violates the image of his mother's tiny, porcelain hands, standing over the ironing board and matching his socks for him when he was a child.

I wish I would have turned my socks right side out.

As the image of his mother dissipates, his anger mounts as he counters his Naysayer. *Yes, they will read my book. It is about the challenges we all face. What I'm writing about lies beneath the mechanics of matching socks, pushing an iron, or placing one foot in*

*front of another to water the desperate and dying plants on my
balcony. I am writing about something more universal, about the
achievement of very small goals, one piled on top of another that will
lead to a bestseller, or a life worth living, or both.*

The next day Steven heads to the office and he receives an email from
a co-worker who works out of Walnut Creek, California.

From: Monica Andrews
To: Steven Sharp
Subject: HELP!!!

Hey Hun! Miss you – Can you please help me get rid of the 3rd page in this
document? So not ok...I am SMRT ☺ LOL! Thank you for any and all assistance
and happy Monday!

Monica

Steven had started calling Monica "Hun" awhile back and now it is a
word they both use to address each other. Steven promises to help
her get rid of the blank page in her Microsoft Word document and
immediately opens the attachment. If you want to know how Steven
was able to get rid of the last blank page in ten seconds or less, follow
him on Twitter @ssharpga.

[That was a joke.]

But following Steven on Twitter is not what this book entry is about.
He takes a look at the email attachment with the blank last page. His
eyes stop darting from side-to-side, the color drains from his face, and
the excitement that lights his eyes fades. Methodically, he removes
the blank last page and sends it back. The attachment describes the
Sandler Sales model's success triangle. The success triangle discusses
the importance of goals, attitudes, behaviors, and techniques – all the
things Steven wants to write about.

Someone has already figured out☺, and most likely written countless books, spelling out a technique, a process for what I want to write my book about.

Is there a value in Steven's having figured this out on his own? His Naysayer starts mouthing off in his head, *What do you really have to add to the mix, if large corporations are having all of their Senior Account Executives learn the Sandler Sales model? Are you merely writing in your own inarticulate way about sales techniques that have worked for all sales people for centuries?*

There are no new ideas, Steven. The voice of the retired, Senior Vice President of Sales for La Prairie and Steven's former manager fills his head. Steven is beaten down, convinced again he will never be more than a frustrated dreamer.

Why are you wasting your time trying to help people, when the help is already out there, and most likely written in a far superior way to the "help" you are offering? Steven thinks to himself as he glances down and looks in the System Tray of his work laptop and sees that it is 4:58 p.m. *Thank God! Time to say "Sharp...OUT!" to my team and get the hell out of here.*

A few days later when Steven has walked away from the idea that he is common, he clicks inside the Notes field of the "Get out of Bed," 6:00 a.m., recurring appointment he set for himself when he was convinced that a regimented schedule was the antidote for leading a life of invisible misery. *Let's see how many of the things associated with this "appointment" I am not doing.*

You get out of bed when you wake up. You do it and you follow the day's plan. You work toward your goals, not someone else's, but your own. Your soul incarnated into your body to learn to do the things you've yet to do. You stay in bed because you are afraid, but **the reality is you have all the courage you need inside of you at the**

moment you refuse to get out of bed. Your excuses are nothing but your fears manifest. **You have the strength and courage to face all of your fears. Get out of bed this second.** You are destined for greatness and not even you can hold yourself back. When you wake up, if it is after 6:00 a.m., you get out of bed and you start your day. You follow your schedule. You move. You accomplish things. You cross things off your list. You embody the qualities you want to stand for. You represent the good, the bad, the ugly, the utter perfection that is you. **You accept yourself wholly and completely: what you like about yourself and what you hate.**

Chapter 7
Everybody Needs a Coach

Steven gets an email indicating Debby Stone is here to see him. Debby Stone is a certified executive coach and owner of Novateur Partners; she is the executive coach with whom Steven works.

[For each coaching appointment, clients are encouraged to complete a "Coaching Prep Form" prior to the day's appointment. Steven includes excerpts from these forms to provide insight into how his coaching relationship with Debby influences and relates to the ideas in this book.]

He goes to the lobby to greet Debby and escort her to the conference room he has reserved. Debby is wearing a taupe wool jacket with black trim, a black skirt, black sheer hose, and black heels. She is petite, has brunette-colored hair she wears in a bob, professionally-applied makeup, and looks really fit.

Debby makes herself comfortable as she and Steven discuss how the coaching relationship will work. Debby switches gears to discuss the values exercise he was asked to complete. "So the values exercise was difficult?"

"Yes, it was tough. I kept coming back to it. I wanted to make sure the values I was selecting were the right values." Steven looks directly at Debby as he responds, and Debby does not look away, not even to blink it seems. *What an amazing listener she is!*

Debby reads Steven's values back to him. "We need to make sure you construct your life honoring your core values...Identifying what your core values are is the first step in that process. We'll come back to these values a lot...Let's review your Coaching Prep Form you completed."

COACHING PREP FORM

How am I doing today?

I am doing OK as far as work goes. I am doing well on my commitment to fitness.

What did I not get done that I intended to do?

I have not written at all for my book.

What are my current opportunities?

Continue to work out at lunch time. Maybe some writing time at my desk after everyone leaves the office?

What do I want to get out of today's appointment?

I want to set some goals.

What issues do I want to focus on in today's appointment?

I want to start getting up earlier. I want to set some goals. I want to find the time to write more. I want to discuss some ideas to make my life less sedentary.

As Debby reviews his completed form, Steven looks out into the parking lot through the brown, dented, conference room mini blinds. What Steven sees is even more dismal than the smudged, smeared "whiteboard" across from him.

"So you want to set some goals? Is that where you would like to start this morning?"

"Sure. Sounds good. I am obsessed with the idea that our goals allow us to be defined by the things we *want* to do, rather than the things we *have* to do."

"Oooh. That's interesting. Let's talk more about that."

After Steven and Debby finish discussing goals and how important he thinks they are, they conclude this session. Steven pulls out his phone and sees that Julie has texted him.

> Checking in with you SS. You bringing me that food journal?

> I sure am.

One of these days, Steven knows he will bring his food journal to Julie so technically it isn't a lie. Steven looks down at his watch. *Oh Shit! I've been cancelling a lot on Dan lately AND I DON'T WANT TO RUN...I don't feel like running today...Maybe if he forces me to run I can trip and fall and scrape my hand real bad to get out of it...This could work....*

"Quick" three mile run day

"We're running today. It's not too hot out yet. Let's run outside. We'll run down to the river and back. It'll be quick." Dan walks past Steven's cubicle.

"Quick?" *Sure it'll be quick. Quick for me to want to dive into the Chattahoochee River and drown myself.* "How quick?"

"Just a little over three miles. I'll come get you at 11:30 a.m. I'll remind you to have a snack around 10:30 a.m., OK?"

"Ummm...I have nothing to eat, so I guess I can't go. Sorry. I really wanted to today," Steven lies.

"No worries. I'll make you a protein shake and you can have an apple of mine."

Chapter 8
Don't be an Endless, Perpetual, Ongoing Reaction

Writing about goals one day

There are goals. They determine where we end up in life, and the absence of having goals brings its own destination.

Steven became a forty-five-year-old man who was completely miserable; he credits his misery, in large part, to the absence of having goals. There were things flying around in his psyche many might label goals, for example, wanting to pay off his mortgage, get out of credit card debt, or wanting to get back into the gym regularly and reclaim the body he had lost. So what differentiates a true goal from wishful thinking?

Goals are measurable; they are attained by constructing them as a series of much smaller, easily achievable destinations. With goals, there are timelines and there is accountability. There is both forgiveness of yourself and honesty with how you are showing up in attaining and moving toward these goals. There are times when you need to tell yourself, "You haven't done crap." This is not an impetus to give up or doubt yourself; in fact, it is the opposite—it is an opportunity for you to strengthen your resolve.

Steven realizes he never had true goals because he didn't have the courage within himself to think he was anything special. His problem was not striving to climb mountains that were too tall, but for passively accepting the bumps in the road that came his way and thinking they were mountains.

Who really knows when change begins? Is it the moment when you physically, noticeably begin to act differently and engage in more positive behaviors? Or is the destruction that precedes the creation where the change starts?

Steven believes change starts with the destruction.

So what is my goal? What are my goals? How do I make these goals different from the wishful-thinking, pipe dreams that simmer in my consciousness?

You write them down, Steven. You write them down. You visualize them in vivid, Technicolor detail. You know your ideas have their own electromagnetic reality. You know your thoughts cause the particles in your proximity to rearrange themselves into the things you think about. You are as sure of this as you are that you will make up one million excuses as to why you don't have to get up tomorrow morning.

As a result of these musings about having goals, Steven creates this goal-setting sheet to help himself clearly define his goals and where he is going in his life.

When using the goal setting worksheet, your long term goals must consider these dimensions of a healthy self. The dimensions of a healthy self are listed in Chapter 9. Investing time and developing interests in multiple dimensions leads to a well-balanced life and a "life portfolio" that can resist the ups and downs and twists and turns that life can throw your way. In much the same way you diversify your stock portfolio and retirement accounts, developing interests and investing your time in several of these dimensions safeguards you against unexpected life changes: divorce, loss of job, a best friend moving away, etc.

Steven's Goal Setting Worksheet

	1	2	3
Long-Term Goals (3-5 years. Outcome based, results focused)			
Interim Goals (3 months to 1 year. Achievable, Outcome based)			
Short-Term Goals/ Daily To Do Lists (Daily to do activities. Behavior based, not result focused)	1. 2. 3. 4. 5. 6. 7. 8. 9.	1. 2. 3. 4. 5. 6. 7. 8. 9.	1. 2. 3. 4. 5. 6. 7. 8. 9.

Your Long-Term Goals

Using the goal setting worksheet takes a little bit of thought. You must first get in touch with the ideas that flow through your mind. The things you daydream about. The things you think about when you can't sleep. These ideas become your long term-goals. They can be far-fetched, stretch goals, the ideas part of you doesn't believe you can achieve.

They are the things that YOU want to do, not what your father thinks you should do, or what your peers think you should do, or what society thinks you should do.

Your long-term goals are results, outcome-focused.

Never forget: the mere fact that you dream about these things for yourself is proof that you can achieve them. It will not be easy. You will have to exorcise your personal demons in most cases. But it is why you came here in the first place: to accomplish the things you are afraid to admit to anyone you dream about and that keep you up at night.

Your Interim Goals

Your interim goals are more realistic and more attainable. They are pit stops on your journey to your longer-term goals. Achieving them will make you happy and experience a sense of accomplishment. They will confirm that you are moving forward, that you are going somewhere. Let's say you weigh 200 pounds and your long-term goal is to weigh 150 pounds with a thirty-two inch waist. An interim goal might be to weigh 165 and have a thirty-four inch waist. Both goals are outcome, results focused.

Let's say you dream of being a doctor. Your long-term goal would sound something like this: "Work in a group practice in my specialty in a large metropolitan area." Your interim goals may be to: (1) complete medical school; (2) apply for and complete residency. You must complete medical school and your residency before you can achieve your long-term goals.

The interim goals you set for yourself later in life (provided you don't use the example of becoming a doctor!) can realistically be achieved in three months to one year. Determining the interim goals can sometimes be the most difficult part, because you know where you dream of being (long-term goals) and you know what you need to do on a daily basis to take you there (short-term goals).

Setting outcome-focused interim goals can be tough; at least it is for me. But, they are necessary.

Your Short-Term Goals

Think of your short-term goals as glorified to-do lists, simple activities that move you closer to your interim and longer-term goals. Your short-term goals are behavior-based, not results-focused. What activities do you need to engage in on a daily basis to become the person who has already achieved your long-term goals?

Short-term goals are very basic. If you struggle with depression or motivation, make these tasks rudimentary, like: get up, make your bed, water your plants, fold the clothes in the dryer, go to the bank, etc. During periods of depression, always create to-do lists and one by one cross items off your list as you accomplish them. The goal is to make your daily tasks inch you closer to your interim goals, ultimately inching you closer to your longer-term goals.

***

When I was in my twenties, my parents asked me what I wanted to do with my life. I thought about it for a moment, and then I made them promise not to laugh at me. Once I had their word, I proclaimed, "I want to be famous."

Dad choked. Mom smiled uncomfortably, but held her composure pretty well for someone who must have been biting her tongue and pinching her ass real hard not to laugh at me.

Mom recovered well, "What do you want to be famous doing? Do you want to act? Sing? Be an interior decorator? A hair dresser or fashion designer?"

[Okay, she didn't really suggest the last three. But probably she was thinking them.]

"I don't know," I said, a tin man-like expression forming on my face.

But I did. I did want to be famous. I do want to be famous. I never mentioned this enduring desire of mine to anyone again. Ever. Not Chris Gorton. Not Michele DiFranco. No one.

Today, Steven sees he will write a series of bestsellers. His iPad® is his new journal and his Livescribe® notebook his new medium that coalesces into physical form the fleeting, ambitious ideas that haunt him and keep him awake at night.

I will be interviewed on talk shows. I may have a reality show, and my viewership will be comprised of all of the other 45, 50, 35-year-olds who have a dream that burns inside of them. Once they see I was able to do it, they will realize they can do it too!

GOALS:

1. *Write your bestselling book(s)*

2. *Workout with weights 5x per week. Build muscle mass; lose fat*

3. *Start dating; find a partner*

4. *I think I want my own talk show*

5. *Have washboard abs*

6. *Pay off all of my credit card debt, short term debt*

7. *Keep my food and exercise journal again*

You need to put these goals into your goal-setting worksheet, Steven. Goals are not goals until you write them down.

Writing about these goals causes Steven to think back to when he was convinced he was going to write his book on artist sketch paper. *Bryan was only nineteen...WOW! That was ten years ago.* He went to Binders Art Supplies and Frames and purchased a sketchpad. At the time, he reasoned he had been unable to realize his dream of being a published author because he was unable to be constantly reminded that he was writing a book. Makes sense, right?

So rather than filling up journal after journal, he decided he would journal in this sketch pad. After filling each page, he would tape it to the walls of his loft, one after another, attempting to write his book. *This is going to look soooooo artistic; it'll look aged, have a shellacked finish and give a paper mache' effect to my walls.* He labeled this technique the "wallpaper your way to a new life" technique as he affixed page after page after page of these disjointed thoughts and intermittent brilliance to the walls of his home, convinced when this art project was done he would have all he needed to be a published author. In retrospect, all this "technique" did was make his house look hideous.

Here I am ten years later and I still don't have a book that has written me out of my present into a future Steven Sharp: a respected, published author and public speaker. Yet my 29-year-old friend has already written and published two books?

All of his attempts to digitalize what he has learned—in all its vivid detail, to take it from the ethereal realm, a place beyond words and verbal reasoning, to a concrete, solid place—have been in vain.

Steven knows that writing down the things that fly through our heads is the way that everything, and he means absolutely everything, comes into existence in our three-dimensional, time obstructed, day-to-day existence. So he plods forward, determined to write down the ideas that exist in his mind.

***

One day Steven sits drinking coffee from the good coffee machine on the third floor at work, from the "Innovation Station," no doubt named this because "innovation" is all the rage in corporate America these days...or at least it was five years ago or so, when he was forced to read *Blue Ocean Strategy* to try and get an e-Learning project for his software training and consulting company.

Steven supposes "innovation" is still relevant, though frankly he could care less what others consider to be relevant. *I guess for those who can only do what has already been done, the focus upon innovating has value. But for me, I won't do so many things because others do, or will, or have; even when we live in a world where there are no new ideas as Vickie Kent, the retired senior vice president has taught me...and I suppose there are no new things to do either.*

Steven continues staring at the ceiling, lost in the world he creates for himself. *But new people can sing old songs, and I guess if you really take a moment to think about this, new people doing old things does in fact make the thing itself new. This is the gist of Heisenberg's Uncertainty Principle: that as an object is perceived, the object itself changes, and I suppose the person changes too. As a person engages in a behavior, the intersection point of everything he has been, thought and everything that action will turn him into, fused together with the zeitgeist of the moment make it new, I suppose. At least in my humble opinion it does.*

So maybe each thought and each action is unique to the thinker or the doer? Who the eff knows at 7:35 a.m. on a Wednesday morning, as Steven sits listening to this amazing YouTube cover of Kelly Clarkson's "Irvine" by petitfleur86. *What I write in this book is earth shattering, at least for me it is, and that is all there really is, Steven. So write, dear Steven. Write.*

Steven takes a break from writing and posts this comment for petitfleur86's YouTube video: "One of my absolute favorite songs of all time. I know Kelly has said she will never perform this song live because she never wants to return to the emotional place where she was when it was written. You have an amazing voice and do a perfect job capturing the feeling of this song. Thank you for posting:)"

You have to give a little back, put a little more out there than you take away; give people the encouragement they may so desperately need so that they have the courage, fortitude, and conviction to keep chasing pavements. *Who is giving me the encouragement? That's a good question, Steven. A very good question.*

Steven continues this conversation with himself and realizes why he can be in a conference room full of colleagues, completely oblivious to minutes and minutes of conversation. He has an awfully active imagination. *I refuse to have my identity determined by the way that others treat me; meaning, that since others don't take the time to tell me that I can be an accomplished author, that I will not take the time to tell someone she can be an accomplished singer. I want Steven Sharp to be the person I (italicized and in all caps) want to be.* **Not an endless, perpetual, ongoing reaction to everything that is lame around me and within those around me.**

Love is a verb, Steven. You have to show people you care; you can't just care. When you just care, it is another discarded thing you have, like an outfit in the back of your closet you never wear. Sometimes you have to put on your Sunday best, or at least a dress shirt and slacks newly pressed from the dry cleaners.

Steven concludes transcribing these ideas that evening and heads to Starbucks on Ponce de Leon. "I'll have a Grande Skinny Vanilla Latte with Whip." He is proud of his ability to order his drink perfectly.

"Hot or cold?"

"Hot."

"I need a Grande Skinny Vanilla Latte with Whip for Steven." The cashier scrawls some instructions on the cup as she passes it to the barista.

I'll always have it hot, even if it's a hundred degrees outside, causing sweat to pour off of me as I drink it. It's a better investment. The cold ones disappear too quickly.

After working on his book for a while he has to use the men's room and notices there is a combo lock on it. He walks over to the barista that he has a weakness for—dirty blonde hair, thick glasses, creamy ivory complexion, incredibly funny, and kind of alternative —and asks, "How does one get into the men's room?"

Without hesitation she responds, "You have to do a dance."

Steven too, without hesitating, puts both arms over his head and tries his best to move how one would to that forties big band type music they play at Starbucks that sounds like it would be from some Fred Astaire movie. His "dance" is a cross between the arm movement one would expect a queen to do at a gay bar in the nineties to some Madonna song, combined with the hip and leg movement one would expect to see from a beginner at ballroom dancing.

"Or you could press one, two, three, four, five," she interjects quickly, shielding her eyes as if she were being assaulted.

"Oh? You don't like the way I dance?

"Just press one, two, three, four, five," she repeats and smiles.

She reminds Steven we have to take time out to dance and have fun.

[Bryan, when he was reading my manuscript as a test reader loved this "scene"...he thought that it showed a burgeoning freedom within me, that my dancing in Starbucks showed I was becoming free of what those around me think.]

Am I becoming liberated from what the people around me think? Steven stops to ponder this for a moment.

Chapter 9
The Dimensions of a Healthy Self

> Hey Michele! Now, it's my turn! I
> haven't heard from you in a while.
> I guess that means you haven't
> completed the inventory of your
> strengths and weaknesses?

Michele receives Steven's text. *How does he know this stuff? I guess the same way I know what is going on with him when I don't hear from him,* Michele thinks to herself. She chooses not to respond.

Steven tries not to focus on Michele and the things she says she wants for herself. Instead, he continues working on his book. He lists the dimensions of a healthy self and describes how he uses Microsoft Outlook to ensure his life invests in these dimensions.

To encourage himself to be intentional about how he spends his time, Steven uses the Category feature in Microsoft Outlook to create a category and color code for each dimension. Next, he creates recurring appointments for himself and assigns a category (color) to each appointment on his weekly schedule. By doing this, his weekly schedule becomes a visual way to ensure that he spends his time wisely in several dimensions (Figure 2).

☐	☐	Career
☐	▣	Exercise/Tennis
☐	▣	Family/Family of Choice
☐	▣	Goals (Long Term)
☐	▣	Hobbies
☐	■	Peer Relationships
☐	☐	Primary Love Relationship
☐	■	Relationship with Self
☐	▣	Self-identity
☐	▣	Service to Community
☐	▣	Spirituality/Religion

In Chapter 2, Steven presented the statistic that anywhere from 70-80 percent of Americans are not fulfilled in their current jobs. And that the typical American watches twenty-eight to thirty-four hours of television per week. If you combine these two statistics and create a schedule for the person who is not satisfied in his current job and watches 4.31 hours of television per day, you get a picture that tells a powerful story (Figure 1).

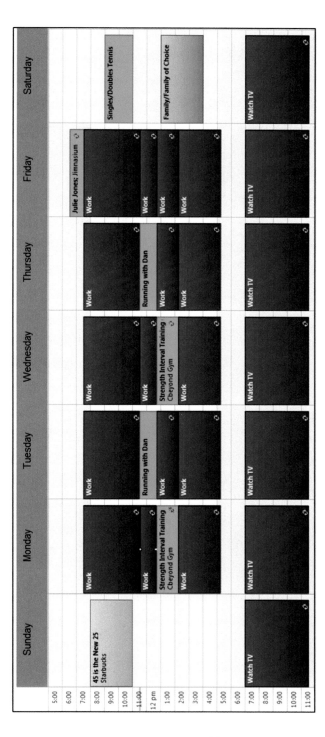

Figure 1. Typical American schedule assumes an individual who is dissatisfied in his current job and an average of 28-34 hours per week spent watching television. The darkness in this schedule represents lost opportunity: Nine hours per day in a job you don't love and 4.31 hours per day watching television, rather than learning a new skill to create new employment opportunities for yourself. Do you want to live a life that is a mere shadow of what it could be? Or, do you want to live a more colorful life?

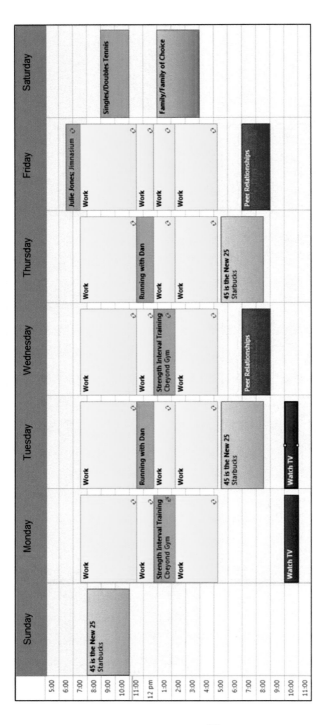

Figure 2. In Steven's weekly schedule, yellow represents a satisfying and fulfilling career, green represents regular exercise, plum represents hobbies, blue represents time spent with family or family of choice. In Section 3, you will be instructed to align your long-term goals with several of these dimensions. Steven's long-term goals center on exercise, career, hobbies, building peer relationships, and family/family of choice.

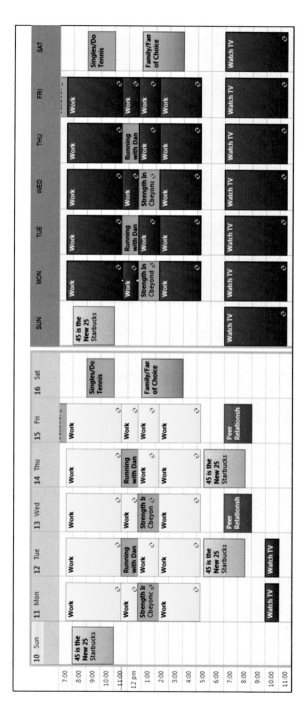

Figure 3. This figure compares the weekly schedule of an individual who is fulfilled at work and who nurtures the dimensions of a healthy self to a weekly schedule of an individual who watches 4.31 hours of television per day and is dissatisfied at work. By watching television as much as the typical American does, what are we sacrificing? What if, instead of watching TV, we invested that time into a future self we wanted to be? In 5.65 years (34 hours a week times 52 weeks) we could be expert in anything we wanted to be. This means any forty-year-old could be an expert in anything by the age of forty-seven.

Super Brain by Deepak Chopra, M.D. and Rudolph E. Tanzi, Ph.D. describe a theory referred to as "10,000 hours." The gist of this theory is that you can become an expert in any skill if you apply yourself for that number of hours, notwithstanding music and art. In fact, the authors of *Super Brain* go on to state that every act/skill in Cirque du Soleil is taught to ordinary individuals who attend a special school in Montreal.[4] These individuals invest the 10,000 hours necessary to become experts and are not legacy to an acrobatic family.

What does the typical American sacrifice by watching so much television? If every hour spent watching television was invested in learning a new skill or investigating a new profession, in 5.65 years, anyone could be an expert in anything (Figure 3).

Steven came across these dimensions of a healthy self one day and saved a copy of it, knowing he would use this concept when he wrote his first book. Basically, if you invest too much of your time and energy into one of these dimensions and this dimension falls apart, you have no buffer in the other dimensions to provide stability in your life. For example, you invest all of your waking energy building your relationship with your significant other at the expense of your own hobbies and peer relationships. If this relationship ends, the part of you who had friends and had hobbies no longer exists.

Steven wished he had invested time and crafted plans to nurture more than a few of these dimensions of a healthy self, because his life had fallen apart once, when his career fell apart, and all he used to unknowingly define himself vanished. He realized it happens to others, too.

Steven's worry for Michele continues to mount as he grabs his phone and texts Michele again.

---

[4] Chopra, Deepak M.D. and Tanzi, Rudolph E. Ph.D. Super Brain, "A Golden Age for the Brain." 2012. P. 6. Print.

I thought you wanted my help, Michele? I want to help you get your life back on track. I think you are so smart. You need some encouragement. There is no judgment here.

Thank you, Steven. I don't want to be a disappointment to you.

Michele, I will never judge you, and you could never be a disappointment to me. Let's talk soon.

Michele helps Steven to realize it is not a matter of wondering whether you will disappoint someone as you try on new behaviors; it is a matter of making it fun to face the challenges we face.

Chapter 10
Make it Fun!

COACHING PREP FORM

What have I accomplished since our last appointment?

> Not writing yet on my book. Thinking a lot about it, but not
> actually doing it yet. I am slowly removing some of the barriers,
> so I know it is going to happen one of these days.

What did I not get done that I intended to do?

> Let's set some specific goals around book writing.

What do I want to get out of today's appointment?

> We have to set some goals or I will never accomplish my book. I
> am getting discouraged, or, rather, I am losing momentum and
> my interest in "being a writer" is starting to wane.

What issues do I want to focus on in today's appointment?

> We need to operationalize the goals I set for myself. For
> example, "Start writing again." While one would think this goal
> is self-explanatory (LOL), it clearly is not. I feel like I need a book
> coach, but I don't even know if there is such a thing.

"Steven, where would you like to start today?"

"I don't know what the eff I am doing with my book. I can't motivate
myself to write. I feel like here I go again, I am going to stop writing,

and I am going to be OK with it, until I'm not. Then I will pick it up and start again."

"You can't motivate yourself to write? Tell me about that." Her calm, confident tenor reaches through the phone and comforts him.

"I keep setting aside time to write, and I keep bailing on myself. I tell myself I can do it tomorrow."

"What is stopping you?"

"I don't know. It's not fun, and I can't make it fun."

Debby reviews the values sheet Steven had completed. "Well, fun is important to you. It is your number two core value. Let's brainstorm ways that you can make this more fun for yourself."

Steven lets out a long, dramatic sigh. "I tried enrolling someone who I work with who is also writing a book to be my writing partner. We wrote together for a few weeks and then that relationship dissipated...I live by myself and once I get home, I want to get on YouTube or listen to music. I can't force myself to open my laptop."

"OK. Maybe you can find a place to write without going home first?" Debby suggests.

Like do not pass Go, do not collect two hundred dollars. "Yeah. Maybe...I keep thinking I need to hire a book consultant, but I don't even know if there is such a thing. I've been wanting to say this to you for a couple of sessions now."

"Well...there is such a thing, and I know two. One is here in Atlanta and the other is in California. Your homework is to contact one or both of them and report back to me."

Is there really an easy solution to every problem? Where do these ideas come from? Who knew there are book consultants in the world?

"OK! I'm in. I will start with the one in Atlanta since I hate to talk on the phone. What's her name?"

"Bonnie Daneker. Her company's name is Write Advisors."

"Can you send me her contact information?"

"I already have. Check your email."

Chapter 11
The Dream I Don't Dare Myself to Dream

From: **Steven Sharp**
To: **Stephanie Thomson**
Subject: **Letter to Stephanie # 2**

Hi Stephanie,

What a great letter. Definitely worth the wait. I feel like I already know you so much better, and you only have sent me one email!! From this point forward, our correspondence is about our lives, not the lives of characters in books that others will read about, but about the challenges, hopes and dreams of real people. Us. You and Me. OK?

Let me tell you about my college experience. College life did not feel fast forwarded for me. It felt like a necessarily evil, a doorway I had to pass through in order to get to where I was going in my life, even though where I was going was not a physical destination, or series of accomplishments; it was a state of self-acceptance I was seeking, and I could not envision it happening at the University of Georgia with the omnipresence of the Greek fraternity boy and sorority girl mindset. To me, this system—perhaps a projection of my childhood experience onto it—was a further manifestation of the haves and the have-nots, the Great Gatsby of the world I grew up in. Mine was the life of the outsider looking in.

I know what I wrote was a complete hot mess and made no sense, but I am still at work and my new idea is that I write for a little while at the end of each day. I had no idea that it would be louder after 5:00 p.m. than it is before 5:00 p.m. Oh well. "Whatevs," as Scott White proclaimed at the Mobile meeting this Tuesday morning at 10:00 a.m.

I almost fell out of my chair.

So anyway, I moved to Atlanta from Bloomfield, New Jersey in 1985 and started at the University of Georgia in August or September. It was a million degrees, and I was a New Jersey boy who grew up in a high school with at least 90% of Italian Americans. Think about a fusion of *Jersey Shore* and *Real Housewives of New Jersey* without lots of money and ostentatious stuff and that's the high school and town I grew up in.

It was more than culture shock starting classes at the University of Georgia in the fall of 1985. It was identity shock, too. As a freshman or sophomore, I had to come to terms with my sexual identity. An identity, it seems all of the boys in Halcyon Park in Bloomfield, New Jersey were much more aware of than I was.

I was just me and my parents encouraged me to "just be myself," and my Dad advised me to "ignore them." He never really knew how mean children can be, I would come to find out as I got older and shared some of my childhood struggles with him. From five years old to maybe the ninth grade, the last year of junior high school, I was myself, and I "ignored them," or so I thought I had. To everyone else I was a "faggot," a "queer," a "sissy."

Thankfully, I can't hear the words or see their faces anymore. These taunts are part of me now; silent, invisible scars buried deep inside of me: titanium bars erected around me, by me, by the part of myself that came to believe that being different was not OK, that it was something to be ashamed of. Over the years I would come to realize that the damage to me had been done, that even though I no longer had to run home from school so others couldn't throw rocks at me, I was still "running home from school" in all of these invisible-to-me ways I didn't understand. So life for me now is about having the courage to be proud of who I am, proud of all of the imperfections, the self-destructive tendencies, the warts, the ticks, the things that make me me.

The dream I don't dare myself to dream is that one day I can learn to feel and connect to others the way they seem to be able to connect to those around them, and to me sometimes. The way that others are able to love, I suppose. Where the love is expressed from the heart and not processed with the mind. Where it is felt and not thought, where it is shown. "Love is a Verb," as John Mayer so aptly has realized. Love is a verb.

I hope all this stuff I share with you helps my new friend to maybe see me with new eyes the next time we meet, and maybe to inspire you to look on the Auburn campus for other "outsiders," those young, inexperienced, perhaps shameful, insecure lesbians and gay boys and offer them your warm, bright smile. Just because, and not for any other reason.

I would be really interested in having you describe more specifically the things that inspire you and the things that make you happy. Maybe describe a specific situation or event?

I hope you are living in the moment, every moment, even the bad ones. I hope you continue to look for ways to be inspired, but also to inspire others. I hope you can continue to give more than you take.

I miss you.

Your friend,

Steven

After Steven finishes transcribing this email to Stephanie into his book, he thinks to himself, *Steven, Michele, Stephanie, Bryan. Real people. Real characters. Real challenges. Real lives.*

I have to figure out how to be the hero of my own story. I have to get control of the food I eat, my weight, how often I exercise; I have to learn what I am doing writing this book.

The ghetto is in your mind, Steven. The ghetto is in your mind, Steven thinks to himself as the image of Phillis Wheatley fills his head.

Steven re-reads Section 1 of his book for the umpteenth time. *My book is getting so good.*

I wish I had someone to send this text to.

SECTION 2
Getting Help with My Book

A reader is part of a writer's life cycle.

Too much cleverness gets in the way of real writing and real thought. Write for your ideal reader, the one who will get everything you say. In writing, perfection is found not in control but in surrendering to the control of the art itself.

—Julia Cameron

Chapter 12
Six Simple Steps to the New You

Dan asks Steven what his book is about, and Steven tries to tell him without going into cardiac arrest as they run.

"You ready?" Dan has his gym bag slung over his right shoulder as he approaches Steven's desk.

"As I'll ever be…We have to stop at my car and get my stuff."

"OK. I'll go with you to make sure you don't get lost between here and the gym."

Dan and Steven always walk the first hundred yards or so out of the parking lot from the office at the start of their runs. They start to run when they reach the sidewalk along the main road leading into their building. As they are walking Dan turns to Steven and says, "Ya know, dude, I don't even know what your book is about."

"Was that a question or a statement?" Steven stalls for a little bit of time.

"Both. Now answer the damn question, Steven," Dan fires back at Steven half-jokingly and serious at the same time. As they begin their run, Dan suggests with a softer tone, "You set the pace for us, OK?"

As they begin jogging slowly, Steven realizes this question is getting easier to answer, "Well, first of all, thank you for asking…it's about a million different things, Dan. In the end, it asks the question, 'can people turn themselves into whatever they want to be regardless of their past experience or how old they are?'" Steven has a thoughtful expression on his face as they round the corner and head toward the Cochran Shoals running trails along the Chattahoochee River.

"Interesting question," Dan lifts his eyes from the road ahead of them and looks up slightly to the sky. "Do you answer it?" A couple of seconds of silence follow. "Better let me know quickly while you can still talk," Dan needles him.

One of the things Steven loves about Dan is his thoughtful nature and ability to engage in an intelligent conversation. Steven would normally say, 'eff you,' if it weren't so true and a waste of the limited oxygen supply he has left. "I answer it for myself. In fact, the whole book, in a way, is my answer to the question...I identify six simple steps people can take...that I am taking...to turn themselves into anything...that is remotely feasible...they want to be." Steven's breathing starts to become more and more labored as he begins to focus on the traffic light at the intersection of Powers Ferry Road and Akers Mill Road. "Let's jog for...a couple of minutes. I'll start...to tell you the six things...at the red light...when I can catch my breath a little."

"No worries, Steven. You're almost there. You're doing great." The traffic light where they get to stop is maybe a thousand yards ahead of them.

As Dan presses the pedestrian button so they can cross over Powers Ferry Road, Steven starts to catch his breath and begins listing the six steps, "First, you write a short narrative of the person you want to be. Basically, you write about the superstar trapped inside of you. Then you identify what is important to you, your values. You write them down, too." The light turns green and they start jogging up a short hill to the entrance to the Cochran Shoals trails.

"OK. That's two things. What are the other ones?" Dan asks as Steven starts to breathe heavily again.

"This is...a lot...easier...when you do...all the talking," Steven struggles to say in between panting. "Next, you define...goals... then you make a...schedule. Give me a sec...."

"Sure. You're doing great. Let's go a little past the quarter mile marker and then turn around." Since Steven is too winded, they finish the rest of the run with Dan doing all of the talking. They talk about the texts and pictures his wife sends to him as his young children acquire new skills and new aspects of their personalities begin to emerge. He talks about the rental property they own, the financial plans he has for his family, and that he can't wait to show him a picture of the dream house he and his wife have chosen for their family.

Steven listens. *Dan's life is SO different than mine.*

"You have a funny look on your face. Are you OK?"

"You're...such...a good...father, Dan."

"Thank you, Steven," Dan responds both humbly and authoritatively.

As they make it up the final hill and back into the parking lot Steven hunches over and puts his hands on his knees.

"You did great, Steven!" Dan commends him for his effort.

As they walk back into the locker room to shower, Steven looks over at Dan with a dripping, beet red face and says, "Number five is you form a team that supports the person you want to be."

A funny look forms on Dan's face. "Am I on your team?"

Steven thinks for a moment and gets a slight edge to his tone, "I don't know. Are you...are you supporting the person I want to be?" Steven and Dan lock their eyes for a second or two. "And lastly, you adapt, learn and move forward, a millimeter at a time toward the person you want to be."

"Sounds like a good, basic, sensible approach," Dan pauses for a second, the funny look on his face morphing into a slightly irritated countenance. "And by the way, I wouldn't remind you to eat, put up with all of your excuses, and drag you out to run if I wasn't supporting the person you want to be."

Duly noted. I know you're on my team, Dan. Guess I just needed you to say it.

"That's why you're practically the captain of my team!"

Chapter 13

Love Can Always Be Felt and it Can Always Be Shown

> How we doing on that food journal? You want to bring it and get on the scale during your next workout?

> I'll get on the scale. That's all I can promise at this time.

> OK. Dan said you are doing great with your workouts. What you eat is more important than how you exercise.

From: Stephanie Thomson
To: Steven Sharp
Subject: Re: Letter to Stephanie # 2

Steven,

Hey!! I have had a really tough semester. I really don't want to focus on it too much, however. A close friend of mine's sister attempted suicide, and one of my roommates has been struggling with heartbreak due to a past relationship. Another roommate struggles with bitterness about many things in her life, including the deaths of two people that she used to be close to.

When something like that happens, suddenly the little things in life seem much less important and those that are close to you seem all the more precious. Processing what has happened and seeing the way it affected those around me was hard for me to deal with. It made me question my own life and how I was living it. What if that had been me? Am I prepared to die? Can I say that I've lived a life I'm proud of?

Enough of all of that... You asked about the things that inspire me... *people* inspire me. People who live their lives in freedom and unashamedly show how much joy they have inspire me. People who stand up for what they believe in inspire me. But most of all, I am inspired when I see people give of themselves to others in order to bless them without expecting anything in return. People giving more than they can take (thank you for those words). That is not a virtue that is looked upon very highly in our world today that is consumed by what seems like a mindset of entitlement.

I want to thank you for sharing your previous struggles with me. I know how hard those are to share, especially when they have cut you as deep as they seem to have. I am so sorry that you've had to encounter the unkindness of this world on so many occasions, but I am so impressed by the way that you've seemingly decided to not let bitterness settle into your soul because of those ignorant people. I find it very admirable that despite the fact that you carry those scars, you have turned those experiences into ones to be learned from.

However, I found myself sad when I read your words on love: "The dream I don't dare myself to dream is that one day I can learn to feel and connect to others the way they seem to be able to connect to those around them, and to me sometimes... Where the love is expressed from the heart and not processed with the mind."

You see, I know I am a hopeless romantic, but I believe that love can always be felt and it can always be shown. When you invest in people by getting to know them or giving them words of encouragement and affirmation, that's love. There are so many ways to give love and show love and *feel* it without it being romantic. And often, I find that that's the type of love that I receive the most joy from. Not only when I am given that type of love, but when I give it to others.

I hope that you are doing wonderfully, and I look forward to getting coffee with you in a week when I'm back at work.

Your friend,

Stephanie

Steven stares up to the ceiling and thinks about making Stephanie sad with his thoughts on love. After a moment or two, he pulls his iPhone out of his pocket and texts Michele.

I need help with this book, Michele. I don't know what I am doing. I emailed this book advisor and she hasn't even emailed me back.

Don't get so frustrated, Steven! She will email you back.

Well if she doesn't, I guess I will have just failed again at this whole grandiose idea that I can be a published author. I don't know what the hell I am doing.

Michele chooses not to reply. *Who am I to reply when I don't know what I am doing with my life either?*

Chapter 14
Don't Watch TV

After arriving home from work and relaxing for a minute, Steven picks up a pair of black, cheap, fake wool Calvin Klein pants he had bought at Marshall's and worn to work that day. *These look like a pair of "dress" pants a waiter would wear with one of those white polyester cotton blazers, complete with permanent food stains around the cuffs.* Next, he picks up a red, faded, short sleeve shirt he had worn with the black pants, and he is reminded he and Dan had dressed similarly that day...well, sort of.

Dan had worn a shiny, red sports-material short sleeve shirt with dark gray dress slacks, perfectly matching gray socks and perfectly polished, black dress shoes.

Even the straight guy in the office dresses better than me, Steven thinks.

Steven's evening ritual
Logitech® Wireless Headsets
Windows Speech Recognition

Steven grabs his headset and starts Microsoft Word. Next, he clicks the Start button, selects All Programs, navigates to the Accessories folder, and starts Windows Speech Recognition.

"Start listening," Steven commands. His Lenovo touchscreen responds, "Listening." *It's starting. I'm using time effectively!* Steven smiles and begins straightening up his house.

Steven continues dictating, "How many times has a person uttered the words, 'I would if I could only find the time or something to that effect'? Steven knew in writing this book, he had to debunk the myth that there was not enough time to accomplish the goals that people set for themselves."

As Steven edits his dictation, he thinks: *It is our job to overcome the made-up barriers we place in our own way until the dream we contemplate has been realized.*

Steven stops for a second to consider this thought.

Easier said than done, since the limitations and obstacles we perceive are both real and many times invisible. We chain ourselves to our own pasts by not realizing we have the keys to unlock the shackles on our feet so we can dance.

When Steven bought his wireless headset, he saw himself on his hands and knees scrubbing the floors, Windexing countertops, polishing his appliances, and folding clothes, all while dictating. Today, he folds all his laundry, picks up his house, packs his lunch, and takes his workout clothes to the car while dictating his book. The dictation isn't perfect, but it is 70 percent of the way there. Julia Cameron, one of Steven's favorite authors, refers to this part of the writing process as "laying tracks."

Steven is no longer merely talking about effective time management; he is managing the time in his personal life effectively. He recalls listening to Joan Tolliver share her life story at a recent company meeting. Joan recounted how she managed two children while finishing college. When she addressed the group, she shared that she could recall cooking dinner for her children. As she stood stirring a pot with one hand, she held flash cards with the other hand. As she stirred, she studied each card until she knew it. She moved that card to the back of the pile and studied the next one.

Meal after meal and flash card after flash card, Joan made her way through college and raised two children. Joan is in her fifties and is currently a senior vice president where Steven works. We execute ordinary tasks everyday like folding laundry, ironing, cleaning out the refrigerator, and if we had the right tools and support system, we can accomplish the things we don't think we have the time to do. Steven uses his evening ritual to straighten his house, dictate his book with his wireless headsets, and to get ready for the next day.

Time Management Techniques That Work

1. Record voice memos for yourself on your smartphone while driving. Make grocery lists, to-do lists, record those fleeting thoughts before you forget them. Transcribe your lists so you can cross things off—builds self-esteem and a sense of accomplishment.

2. Use a speech-to-text app on your smartphone to help transfer your handwritten ideas to digital form. (Saves you the trouble of having to type.) Takes a while to get used to, but works nonetheless.

3. Get wireless headsets so you can multitask efficiently. Talk on the phone using Skype while you perform routine household chores. Strengthens friendships and gets your chores done at same time.

4. Use your wireless headsets to work out while dictating. Having the body of a twenty-five-year-old is much more difficult when you are past forty-five. You can work toward more than one goal at a time. Lose weight and write a bestselling book. Build muscle and read interesting articles.

5. Don't have a TV that works. Or don't watch the one you have that does work. Watch TV on demand via Netflix or Hulu Plus. Television has many drug-like effects. Turning off the TV may make you realize you have no hobbies, that you have nothing you enjoy anymore.

(Be prepared to go through a phase where you don't know what to do with all of the time you have when you no longer are mindlessly watching TV. Discover things you enjoy. Create a life for yourself that entertains you. You can do it. I did. I *am* doing it; for a period of time, be willing to accept the fact that you have nothing you enjoy in your life that's just for you and that you have nothing you look forward to that is just for you. Turn off your TV. Get in touch with the ideas that fly through your mind. Turn these things you think about into long-term and interim goals and daily to-do lists that move you a molecule closer to the person you think about becoming.)

6.   Get to work thirty minutes before you are expected to start working. Chip away at a long-term goal you have set for yourself that you "don't have the time" to accomplish. Do this more days than not. Or, use this time so that you can take a thirty-minute walk over lunch time, transitioning your increasingly sedentary life to one that has more movement in it.

7.   Pack your lunch every day. Eat at your desk so that you can use your lunch hour to work out, to read a book, to play Bridge, to email friends, to write in your journal, to explore new music, to stay abreast of new thinking in your field. Use this time to build your social network, post to LinkedIn or Twitter.

8.   While cooking dinner for your family, quiz yourself with flash cards. Saves money and saves time.

Steven finishes typing the time management techniques and takes out his phone to text Michele.

> Hey Michele,
> I am so excited!! Bonnie, that book advisor I told you about, finally emailed me back!!!!

> That's great, Steven. I knew she would. What are the next steps?

> Not sure!!!!! I will definitely let you know, though. Thank you so much for supporting me and agreeing to be in this book, Michele. The only other person who has [agreed to be in the book] is someone I have known for less than three months.

Jason's Fit 360x class

"You ready?" Dan asks skeptically.

"I am in the middle of something I want to finish," Steven replies.

"You're always in the middle of something, Steven. C'mon. Let's go. Work will be there when you get back."

"OK, give me a second...What hell do you think Jason has in store for us today?" Steven slings his workout bag over his shoulder as they walk past the copy machine.

"Dunno. I'm kind of in the mood for some burpee pullups though." Dan opens the door for them and they walk to the gym together.

In the mood for some burpee pullups?!? Yeah, I'm kinda in the mood to go clubbing with my mother.

"Yeah! Me too. Burpee pullups are great," Steven responds.

Chapter 15
A Week Snow Skiing in Colorado

Hey Michele,
I am meeting my book advisor
tomorrow! She told me the stuff I have
submitted so far is excellent!!! Her
words, not mine☺

Good luck! I know it will go
well

Steven puts his phone away and completes his coaching prep form.

COACHING PREP FORM

How am I doing today?

Doing great. Three workouts in three days. Eating better.

What have I accomplished since our last appointment?

Met with Bonnie Daneker on Monday morning to discuss book. Been working out pretty regularly.

What did I not get done that I intended to do?

Not always leaving work at 5:30 p.m. like I promised.

What are my current challenges?

I want to talk about my meeting with Bonnie and the direction she sees for my book. It is basically the choice between doing something self-indulgent and something more practical.

What are my current opportunities? What do I want to get out of today's appointment? What issues do I want to focus on in today's appointment?

I want to discuss my book project. I want to discuss my book project. I want to discuss my book project.

"So I see you want to discuss your meeting you had with Bonnie, the book advisor I referred you to," Debby chuckles slightly.

"Oh?!? You were able to figure that out from my coaching prep form?"

"Yes. Loudly and clearly." Debby emits a soft chuckle.

"Well...I had originally wanted to write a book that would write a gay man into existence who accepts himself wholly and completely. Of course, that gay man would have been me." Steven pauses for a long moment and continues. "Bonnie and I decided that my first book should have a more universal appeal. We both felt it would be a better business decision to not pigeonhole me as a writer."

"That makes a lot of sense, Steven. How do you feel about the decision you and Bonnie made?" Debby's voice softens slightly.

"I think it is the right decision, Debby."

Steven and Debby conclude their coaching session after a lengthy discussion about Steven's meeting with Bonnie. Steven stays in the conference room he has booked for his coaching appointment and quickly composes an email to Stephanie.

From: **Steven Sharp**
To: **Stephanie Thomson**
Subject: **Hi!!!!!!!!! Remember me??**

Hi Stephanie,

How are you? How have you been? I guess I showed you who could wait the longest to reply to an email message!

So my book project has stalled slightly. I haven't really written much on it since early November – four months. WOW!! So I had this idea that I needed help writing the book, and I was always constructing all of these ways I could get people in my life to help me to write the book. Then sixty pages into the book, I had no idea where the book was going or how I was going to be able to take the reader on a journey with me.

Not even I wanted to read the book I was writing.

Then I got this great idea that I needed to hire a "book consultant." Of course, I had no idea if there even was such a thing as a book consultant, but I shared this idea with my executive coach, and sure enough, there is such a thing as a book consultant!!!!!

Originally, I thought I would be signing a Statement of Work that would be for $3,600, the approximate cost of a week skiing in Colorado. Plopping down the money would be a definitive statement to me that I believed in myself. That I deserved to be a published author, that all the scars inside of me, I didn't let kill me. I used them to make me stronger.

I had discussed this with Debby my life coach and was sure that tomorrow was the first day of the rest of my life (again). I opened the Statement of Work last night and scanned through it until I got to the cost. So anyways, here is the total cost included in the Statement of Work:

TOTAL COST ESTIMATE

Project Management of Composition and Production	$3,600
Book Layout and Design	$2,000
Book Cover Design	$1,000
Book ISBN and Barcode	$ 185
E-Book Creation and E-ISBN ($350, $150)	$ 500
Book Line Editing (@$60/Hr., 12.5 Hrs. Total)	$ 750
Copyright	$ 100
Approximate Printing Costs (Estimate/50 books @ $8)	$ 400
Estimated Total	$8,535

Isn't her Word table formatted horribly???? LOL. Anyway, now I don't know what to do and I meet with her tomorrow. I am not going to boil the ocean over this email. I know it is a rambling hot mess, but I wanted to write to you and let you know I was thinking about you. I also wanted to thank you for opening up to me about how difficult your fall semester was. I hope this semester is easier, with fewer emotional challenges and that you are having fun in college, Stephanie.

Take care of yourself and hope to hear from you soon.

Steven

Quarter mile intervals on the treadmill

"What are we doing today?" Steven asks, already knowing the answer.

"It's Tuesday, Steven. Quarter mile intervals on the treadmill. Same as we always do. Only six fast ones and six slow ones and then you're done. Next week we will do seven. Stop pretending like you don't know what we do on Tuesdays."

Just six fast ones and six slow ones.

Chapter 16
Steven Signs Book Contract

Steven receives an unexpected text from Stephanie

> Hey! Question: what is your address?

> [Steven provides his address.] I signed the book contract today!!!!!!!!

> Yay!!!! Congrats!! So happy for you:)

> Since I am such a MS Word aficionado, I was able to take $2,000 off the cost!!!!!!! So it is only going to be (only) $6500. LOL I am so excited.

> Hey, that's better than nothing!! Looking forward to your next letter:)

After reading Stephanie's text, he receives a welcome text from Bonnie Daneker of Write Advisors.

> Hi Steven,
> Welcome to the Write Advisors' family of clients. We're pleased to be working with you on this impactful project. I was pleased to find that no working manuscript out there (or published) exists that I can find for the "45 is the new 25" title. Let's go with it!

> Hi Bonnie,
> I reserved/bought 45isthenew25.com a few minutes ago. Have a great day!!

Thursday, March 24, 2013
Starbucks on Peachtree and 7th ST
6:40 a.m.

Steven starts writing the date, time, and location on the first three lines, preparing to take notes for his first, in-person meeting with Bonnie.

"How are you, Bonnie? You look just like the picture you sent me." Bonnie is tall, blonde, well dressed, and wears glasses.

"I'm good," Bonnie's calm morning voice is soothing to hear at 6:45 a.m., the time they have decided they will meet each week.

After exchanging small talk, Steven starts signing the paperwork that Bonnie has prepared for him. "So one year from now I will have a completed book in my hands with a cover and everything?"

"Yes. The project management schedule will take one year to fulfill."

"That is pretty exciting! Twenty years before today I have dreamed of being a published author and one year from now it will happen."

"Yes. One year from now you will be a published author." Bonnie asks for Steven's address and she recognizes the neighborhood. "Is that sushi restaurant still there?"

"Gekko? Yes, it is still there. I haven't tried it though."

"I haven't either. I have a friend who likes it...but she's from Wisconsin...so who knows," Bonnie states rather confidently as she gives Steven this look that says, "If, of course, you can trust someone from Wisconsin to know anything about sushi!"

Bonnie changes the subject, "We need to start discussing the themes of your book."

"I really like the spreadsheet you shared with me from your other client. I was struck by how many of the things she wanted to discuss in her book are the same things that I want to discuss in my book. Are these the things that people want to write about?"

"Exactly! These are universal themes, and her take is kind of from a yoga-centric, medicinal kind of approach, where yours is more social and cultural, I think."

"What did you say? From an abysmal kind of approach?"

"No, medicinal point of view," Bonnie laughs out loud. "She used to write for the Jewish Women's Times and she was a blogger. Your book is going to be different than hers because it is going to span a period of time where you see the development of your main characters. We have to be organized about it so we don't lose our reader."

"OK."

"You introduce a character with a challenge. The reader gets it, and then you can give him or her another challenge. Then you introduce another character with a different challenge. The reader gets it, and then you go back to the first character."

Steven jots down the key points Bonnie shares with him about constructing his book. "What did you think about my belief that your thoughts are at the causal level for all physical reality in your life?"

"I love it, and there is a lot of material out there, a lot of scientific research that proves that your belief system is what creates your life. It can hold you back or it can propel you forward."

Steven's lips expand ever so slightly as Bonnie says 'I love it.' "I want to include something that still resonates with me from the book *Ageless Body, Timeless Mind* by Deepak Chopra; he proves that people in their eighties can still develop muscle mass. The book debunks the idea that our bodies decline once we retire. It really is not true, nor substantiated by studies. We start to decline because of the ideas we hold about aging and what we do or no longer do with our bodies. People believe they will start to decline when they reach a certain age, let's say forty-five, for example."

Steven makes eye contact and briefly winks at Bonnie. "Deepak already taught me I can have the body of a twenty-five year old, provided I change my thoughts about aging."

"That is really interesting, Steven. I love it. Let's put it in there somewhere."

Steven switches gears, "Michele wants to learn how to craft her résumé and she wants to know how to leverage her life skills learned from raising a family and how to make it relevant for a job. She wants me to talk to recruiters in various industries, asking what they are looking for." After discussing what Michele's demographic would want in the book, Steven hands Bonnie the list of themes he wants to discuss.

Bonnie scans the list Steven has given to her. "Sure we will fit these themes in. We could say stuff like Julia Childs started cooking at fifty-one; Grandma Moses started painting when she was eighty-three. And I came across this video of an eighty-six-year-old gymnast who performs on the parallel bars and floor exercise."

"How do you know these things?" Steven blurts out.

Bonnie starts laughing, "I am a walking answer key to a Jeopardy board." Bonnie returns to the list of themes as she points to the stuff Michele wants to know about the résumé. "This is where Stephanie's voice can come in, she can be interviewing and she can say something like my recruiter told me, 'whether you are twenty-five or sixty-five, you need to have this, this and that on your résumé,'" Bonnie pauses for a second. "Talk to me about this theme, the evolution of communication."

"OK. At one point, I was obsessed with the evolution of communication. In the 1700s, you had Paul Revere's ride announcing the British were coming. Then you had letter writing, Morse code, radio, telephone, television, mobile phones, text messaging, instant messaging, Facebook, and Twitter. In a way, communication has sped up exponentially, and at the same time, the distance between us could not be greater. I don't know if it fits, but that is what that theme means...I am really excited...not sure if you can tell?" Steven confesses.

"I like the smiles. I like the laughs...We need to figure out how all of these things you want to talk about can fit into a cohesive whole."

Steven notices it is 7:45 a.m. and time to head to work. "You'll help me figure it out. I have a good feeling about this."

"Well… that is my job!" Bonnie smiles brightly and says goodbye as Steven heads to his car.

1:1 personal training session with Julie Jones when she introduces the burpee matrix

"Today, we are going to start this round of exercises with a burpee matrix," Julie announces to Steven.

"If it's anything like the leg matrix, I'm out!"

"Ohhhhh, Steven," a patronizing twinkle forming in her clear blue eyes. "It's much better than the leg matrix. Besides Kristian commented you are starting to look really fit." Kristian is Julie's husband and co-owner of Excellence in Exercise.

Julie begins explaining the burpee matrix as she demonstrates the matrix with two of each exercise. "You take the burpee exercise and break it down into four parts. You put your hands on the ground and you jump your legs back so you are in the plank position. You do this eight times. From the plank position, you do eight push ups. Then you jump your feet forward eight times so your feet are right outside of your hands. You do that eight times. Lastly, you jump up eight times…You ready?"

Yeah, I'm ready. I'm ready to slap that smug look off your face.

"WOW! I haven't seen that dirty of a look in a while. I guess the burpee matrix is here to stay."

Chapter 17
It's Happening

Wednesday, March 27, 2103
Starbucks on Peachtree and 7th ST
6:45 a.m.

"Uhhh...so what day is today? Wednesday..." Steven mumbles with a tone that suggests he isn't quite so sure, still half asleep as he begins scrawling the date, time, and location in the upper left hand corner of his notebook.

"Yes. Today's Wednesday the twenty-seventh," a calm, reassuring tone in Bonnie's voice.

Steven continues mumbling "Uhhhhhh. Oh my God! I wanted to cancel on you so bad this morning...Or badly," Steven immediately corrects himself as he plops down a print out of chapters one and two on the small round bistro table.

"No problem. I understand. I know it's early," Bonnie hesitates slightly, "I think this time slot does work...It may be hard a little bit." There was this thoroughly unconvincing tone in Bonnie's voice, trying to convey to Steven that meeting at 6:45 a.m. at Starbucks every Wednesday wasn't that early.

"So what are we doing?" Steven inquires with more of a commanding tone in his voice, as he starts to wake up.

"So let's jump right into what you've shown...I LOVE the formatting; I love the margins; I love the styles you're using; I love the bubbles. I think you are on your way. And the idea is...keep going."

Bonnie sounds sincere and enthusiastic. *I guess for $6,500 she should.*

"You're doing a great job of not self-editing. I realize you are very careful about what you presented to me. I told you about this exercise. We have to start wide and then narrow it down. Perfect it. And then give it to the audience."

Steven scrawls down key words as Bonnie continues, "I have to ask you from a plot perspective: Does Michele still need money for school?"

"Yes, she does."

"Or, did she go?"

"No. She still needs money for school."

"Well you tell her to go to www.emergescholarships.org and to apply. Tell her I am on the board and we award it for women whose education has been interrupted and they want to go back to school to finish their education. She needs to prove that she gives back to the community. She doesn't have to pay it back. She could at least take five to ten credit hours. Ask her to tell you when she does apply so that I can be on the lookout for the application."

Steven pauses and thinks for a second, "Well that's kind of good...you're already invested in the characters in the book."

Bonnie chuckles. "It's true. It's absolutely true. Oh my gosh. I love this piece here where you are mimicking her mom."

Steven tries to suppress his pride that he has written something that makes someone laugh. "You liked that! You thought that was funny?"

"Yes. I love this. In this one little part, I already know who Michele's mother is: she's negative; she's got this New Jersey attitude. These are counter personalities that will help to solidify your points and define who you and Michele are in contrast to who her mother is."

Steven scrawls furiously. *It's happening*, Steven thinks, as he hurries to write down the words Bonnie is sharing with him, even though the pen is capable of capturing every word, every nuance of the conversation.

"So you know who Michele's mother is from this one little exchange?" Steven fishes to get Bonnie to say more good things about his writing.

"Yes. Absolutely. It makes Michele's character stronger because she has to fight her mother…."

"Well, she has to fight her whole family."

Transcribing these conversations is slow going. People talk so much more quickly than you can capture the words, pauses, changes in inflection, the cadence, the ebb and flow of true conversation: the emotion, the joy, the spontaneity that explodes when two people connect through something they love.

Steven is reminded of that line from the movie *The Hours*. Ed Harris' character tells Clarissa, Meryl Streep's character, that the written word will always pale in comparison to the myriad of things that happen all at once in real life: the sounds, the words, the tone, the gestures, one's posture, clothing, facial expressions, hair style. And this does not include all of what happens on the inside: one's thoughts, doubts, fears, all one has been and dreams of being, the things that can contradict or substantiate all that is observed.

As Steven listens to and transcribes the audio from this session, he finds himself mesmerized by the conversation about this book, about these characters, about the plot, about the character arcs of Michele, and of himself. He stops typing and gets lost in the world of this recorded conversation. He knows he should be transcribing, but can't stop listening.

"With your dialogue, remember, people don't always talk in full sentences. You can interrupt each other," Bonnie offers. "And people finish each other's thoughts."

"Well it was funny because you should have seen me trying to figure out how to get this authentic-sounding dialog. I had the wireless headsets on. Michele would talk a million miles a minute, and I would have to repeat it so my voice was talking into the microphone on the headset so my computer would capture the speech to text recognition. So she would say something, and I would have to say, 'Wait! Wait! Wait!' and try to repeat back everything she had said.

"Words would appear on the computer in fits and spurts. Michele would be listening as I did my best to repeat what I had heard into my headset microphone. Michele would wait until I was done and respond with an emphatic, 'Yes!' Then she would keep going; each time she continued she would talk a little faster and with a little more anger in her voice."

"Can you get her a headset?"

"Well…"

"I know who I am working with here; she can't even get her printer working," Bonnie quickly reminds herself.

"OK. OK. OK. So is this what we do? I submit chapters to you; you review them and give me ideas?"

"Yes. That's exactly what we do. You did a great job of introducing Michele. She's panicked. She loves her kids. She's alone in terms of support, except for you. She has a dream, but its fading. She's forty-five."

"Do you get all of that from this?"

"Yes. Absolutely."

"Because when I read all of Chapter 1 back to her, she was completely silent on the phone and all I had done was transcribe our actual conversation. She said, 'Steven, I am so depressed.' And when I asked why, she said, 'Because that is exactly what my life is like.'"

Steven's voice starts to break a little bit as he relays this interchange to Bonnie and he begins to understand the desperation and futility Michele must experience on a day in and day out basis. He replaces his choked up tone with a smirk, snort, and a chuckle, "So I told her, I thought it was good that she was so depressed hearing it, because then the audience of this book would be able to understand the place she has found herself in at this stage of her life."

It isn't that Steven is being insensitive to Michele; he always sees the bigger picture. On one level, he and Michele's lives together are now the stuff of characters, plots, venues, challenges, and character arcs. The ups and downs of their lives are now the plot twists and turns of his book.

Bonnie's gaze starts to focus on something. Steven glances at the page she's reading and reacts. "Oh...I dumped that in there to see if I can convince you to embrace another theme that happens in the book."

"Yes?"

Steven chuckles a little bit. "Well you didn't jump on it when I first emailed you about it...the theme is me learning how to write the book. I need you to be this New York bitch editor like from *The Help*." Steven can't get it all out without cracking up and Bonnie starts to laugh too. "And I need you to say, 'Steven! This sucks. No one wants to read this...And over here....'"

"I will definitely do that if we need it." Now she is laughing too. "So far we haven't had a reason for me to say that. But I will definitely do it. My name is on this project now too. So I want a certain level of quality."

"So does that mean you are agreeing that I can use your name?"

"Yes. This is going to be a good book. So, yes."

Steven reaches his hand across the bistro table and shakes Bonnie's hand. "I think once you help me build this book on a foundation that is poured with concrete…."

"You can build a mansion…I have no doubt in my mind that you can do that."

Steven loves the idea of his book being a mansion.

Chapter 18
Any Amount of Support Makes a Difference

On his way up to his home one day, Steven finally remembers to collect his mail and is surprised to find a letter from his friend Stephanie. *Why would Stephanie be writing me a letter, rather than emailing me?* Steven thinks to himself as he rips open the envelope.

Dear Steven,

I'm writing to update you a bit about what's been going on in my life recently. In May, I am going on a mission trip to Haiti. We are hoping to take about 20 students to Port Au Prince, Haiti. We will be there the week of May 5th-12th. The mission of this school is to provide an excellent Christian education to impoverished Haitian children and raise educated Christian leaders in Haiti. I'm really excited for the opportunity to serve the Lord alongside my friends, in a country where there is great need.

So first, I would like to ask you to keep the team and me in your thoughts as we embark on this journey. I've never been on an international mission trip and this is my first time outside the country.

I also would like to ask if you would consider supporting me financially on this trip. The cost is $985, plus vaccinations and supplies. I am working to raise the money through the support of family and friends. I know that raising this amount of money is a difficult task, but I know that the Lord provides and that he will come through if I am meant to embark on this journey with him.

If you would like to support me on this trip, please know that any amount makes a difference! Every dollar donated will be used to cover lodging, travel costs and team expenses.

Your prayers for safe travels, willing hearts, capable hands and flexible attitudes will be greatly appreciated! Thank you so much for considering this. It means so much to me!

Sincerely,

Stephanie

Tears stream down his face as he imagines how *sincerely* and earnestly Stephanie has written this letter. And he is angry with himself for not having retrieved his mail sooner. *Stephanie will obviously think I have abandoned her and am not willing to support this journey she will be undertaking in about a month's time.*

Steven is on his way to play tennis and does not have time for a thorough reply, and at the same time, wants time to stop so his reply to Stephanie is not further delayed.

> Hey! I never check my mailbox. I just got your letter. I only scanned through it. I will definitely help. Let me see what I can afford, OK? And, read your whole letter....Off to play some tennis.

> Aww thanks Steven! So actually, I've already met my goal with donations to cover the cost of the trip, so now all I really need are small donations for supplies and my immunizations. So don't worry about shelling out a lot of money or anything!

> How much will your supplies and immunizations cost?

> I'll calculate everything out and I will let you know!

Chapter 19
I am Becoming an Author

> You are not going to see the weight loss you want to see unless I can review what you are eating and when you are eating it.

> I know. And, I have only lost four pounds, and I am working out consistently and pretty hard.

> I know you are. That's why I need to see your food journal.

Wednesday, April 10, 2013
Starbucks on Peachtree and 7th ST
6:35 a.m.

"You look like you have lost some more weight," Bonnie greets Steven.

"Yeah. A little. I am moving it around I think. My arms are getting bigger. I am losing this a little," Steven points to his waistline. "I am definitely trying."

"I see a lot more definition in your face, too," Bonnie adds. Later on, Steven Googles whether a comma is needed in this sentence and decides since it is the voice of his book advisor, he should include it.

"You do? Really? Honestly?"

"Yes, honestly."

"Awwwwwweee. That's what I wanted to hear. So, let's talk about the book...."

"Definitely. I was going to ask you about your goal sheet." [Editor's note: Bonnie's goal sheet is different than Steven's.]

"Well I'm...What's the difference between a quantitative and qualitative goal?"

"Quantitative is numbers."

"So like I want to sell 500,000 books?"

"Yes. And that is probably unrealistic."

Steven starts cracking up.

Bonnie hedges a little and laughs too. "Well for right now. Just so you know, 15,000 is considered a success. 500,000 is absolutely doable if you go at it from a full-blown marketing perspective."

"So how many books do you have to sell to be on The New York Times Best Sellers list?" Steven continues, completely nonplussed.

"About 100,000."

"So if I need to sell 100,000 books to be on the list, I would say that is a quantitative goal, to be on The New York Times Best Sellers list," Steven announces to Bonnie.

"But to sell that amount you have to start to think about groups of individuals who will buy your book: church goers, social workers, stay-at-home moms...."

"OK. So anyway what are we doing today?"

"Well first of all, I love the quote in the beginning of Section Two by Julia Cameron. You don't write a book for yourself, you write it for everyone else, your ideal reader."

But I am writing this book for myself, hoping the things I struggle with are the things everyone struggles with.

"What we were missing before today was an overarching framework which now we have. Project management techniques work. You can still achieve your goals, regardless of your age."

"Yes! That is exactly the book I want to write," Steven exclaims, somewhat distantly aware he has no unpaid person in his life with whom to share the things important to him.

"Steven, I have no doubt you can write *that* book. You're becoming an author," Bonnie responds authentically and enthusiastically.

"Really?" Steven writes, *I am becoming an author.* "Do you really think I am becoming an author?"

"Yes. I really do. Your psychology changes and the things you share change. The magic in writing is giving lots of clues to the reader, but you have to let them come to their own conclusions."

"So you can't tell them certain things?"

"Well you have a balance between that. The magic is the 'AHA!' moment when the reader thinks to herself, 'I finally understand what he is trying to say.'"

"So I was having doubts about what I was going to do with the character of Stephanie and then I received this letter from her." The paper crinkles as Steven pulls out Stephanie's letter about her upcoming mission trip to Haiti.

"Great. I'd love to talk to her about that. I have traveled all over the world and I have seen things in Haiti I have never seen before: the tent villages, the dysentery and the typhoid. The eating on the streets right next to where someone has defecated." Bonnie pauses for a few moments to regain her composure and then continues.

"It's so bad and it's still damaged from the hurricanes and the earthquakes. The Dominican Republic is lush and green and prosperous, and in Haiti you see the rock, where it has been deforested, the poverty. You can see it from the air and then when you get there you can feel it. Haiti is so desolate. They have been stepped on and punched and kicked so many times. I will not be going back to Haiti."

Chapter 20
A Huge Muffin Top and Fat Ass

From: Steven Sharp
To: Stephanie Thomson
Subject: Your Trip to Haiti

Dear Stephanie,

In basic agony today. Hurt my lower back on Friday at the gym doing squats with massive 25 pound plates on each side:-) That's not massive in case you didn't know. Girls squat with more weight than that.

Anyways, it's most likely been six months since I have written to you and you have been on a mission trip to Haiti. I'd love to hear about your trip and tell you what has been going on with my book project.

I have been focused on the book and making good on my investment to my book advisor. I have also been getting my 25-year-old body back. No one wants to see a 45-year-old who is proclaiming that 45 can really be the new 25 with a huge muffin top and fat ass.

In a way, this letter is my apology for having taken so long to write back to you and trying to figure out what to do about my back. It feels ok if I don't move. LOL.

One final note, I had asked a lot of people in my life to help me with this book, people who have known me for a really long time, and you and my friend Michele were the only ones who cared enough about the things that were important to me to help.

Your friend,

Steven

P.S.

Tell me about school, about your experience in Haiti, how it strengthened your convictions or taught you new things, insights it provided to you. I'd love to hear about the impact of this mission trip on who Stephanie Thomson is.

Steven is happy to work out

A few days later Steven's back is feeling basically back to normal as Dan stops over to his desk. "You coming today?" Dan asks with this disapproving, challenging tone in his voice.

"Yes!" Steven answers immediately.

"What do you mean, 'Yes'? I don't have to remind you to eat first or give you a fifteen-minute dissertation as to what I have planned for us today?" Dan asks sarcastically.

"Nope. I'm ready. Let's go!"

Chapter 21
I Can Be Anything I Want to Be

Steven arrives at the Corner Bakery on Peachtree Street about fifteen minutes early and uses the time to prepare for his interview with Debby Stone, his certified executive coach. As he reviews his interview questions one last time, he finds himself thinking about a conversation he had with his mother when he was in his early twenties after he graduated college.

"Mom, how do you know if you are happy?" Steven asked one afternoon way before he had decided that the meaning of life for him is to be happy.

"Steven, ever since I was a very little girl, I only wanted three things out of life. I wanted to be a nurse, I wanted to get married, and I wanted to raise a family," his mother responded earnestly. "I have always been a nurse, and although the medical profession has changed a lot recently, I love my job. I have been married to the same man my whole life, and I have three beautiful children. I'm happy."

"It's different for me, Mom. I am a guy. I didn't grow up in the 1940s and 1950s where women could be nurses or teachers or secretaries. I can be anything I want to be." Steven opened up to his mother, totally unclear as to what he wanted to do with his life.

"You'll figure it out, Steven. I have faith in you."

Thanks for the great advice, Mom. They finished eating lunch, talking about how great the food was and which dessert they wanted to split. Even today, Steven can still feel the restaurant's white tablecloth under his forearms and how much he loves his mother.

Debby Stone Interview Part 1:
Honoring your core values determines
success in life

Steven waves to Debby as she opens the door and he stands to greet her. After they are both seated and exchange pleasantries, Steven begins the interview. "Let's start with your undergraduate education?"

"Public Policy major."

"Because you knew you wanted to be an attorney."

"I thought I wanted to be an attorney. I worked a couple of years after undergraduate hoping I would find something I really wanted to do so I wouldn't have to go back to school. I didn't find anything that I really wanted to do so I went back to school."

"How did you look for something you really wanted to do?"

"Not very well...I essentially took the job with the highest pay and the highest prestige. And, on the surface, it looked like a really good job, and it was a really good job for a lot of people, just not for me. I am not a numbers person, and I became an associate consultant at a management consulting firm, Bain & Company...."

"You're saying you selected a job that wasn't in alignment with your core values."

"Correct. Nor was it in alignment with my actual skills, and I didn't know that either. It was much more spreadsheet-focused than what was good for me."

"Which made it a worse fit: the spreadsheet nature of the job, or it not being in alignment with your core values?"

"Ooooh. That's a really good question...there was a lot about the job that was good for my values, but in the end, not being able to be good at the job meant that it failed one of core values, which is around mastery. I simply wasn't that good at the job."

Steven nods in understanding. "Not a great experience in your first job so you went to law school?"

"Basically, yes. I got accepted at two schools. I aimed very high. I applied to Harvard, Stanford, Columbia, Berkeley, Duke, and UGA and got into Duke and UGA. I decided to go to Duke."

Steven leans forward, resting his arms on the table. "Did you pass the bar on your first try?"

"I did."

"How many law firms recruited you?"

"I lost count...and I am not bragging."

"*Brag! Toot Your Own Horn Without Blowing It,*" Steven coaxes Debby, quoting back to her the book she recommended he read.

"I probably flew to visit with at least a dozen different firms all across the country and could have flown to visit others."

"Impressive." Steven raises his eyebrows and lets out a soft whistle.

"I had very good success with interviews."

"So let me flash forward...sixteen years as an attorney?"

"Yes, basically. After my son was born, I became what I have labeled an 'accidental entrepreneur.' I left my first firm and when I was taking care of my son, friends started to ask me if I could do legal work for them. The next thing I knew I had my own firm. So I was my own boss."

"What did you call it? An accidental entrepreneur? Is that your term?"

"Yes. That was all mine," Debby states matter-of-factly and continues. "So then in the early 2000s I came to basically believe that anyone that said they loved their jobs, I thought they were basically full of it."

"Really?"

"Yes, because I never had a job I loved, so I figured all of those people that said 'I love going to work' were full of it."

"So you would have thought I was lying if I told you I loved to work?" Steven asks, stunned.

"Yes. Until I was more enlightened...."

"Interesting."

"Because I had never done a full-time job that I really enjoyed. I mean they were OK; I could pay the bills, but I certainly never looked forward to Monday. And I didn't really get excited about my job...So I really thought those people were putting on the happy face."

Steven couldn't believe what he was hearing. This person sitting across from him was light years away from the woman she was describing. Steven looked down at the questions he had prepared and tried to regroup.

"OK. Ummmm....So in the early 2000s when you thought that people who liked their jobs were full of crap, if you had to rate your satisfaction with your professional life on a scale from 1 to 10, how would you rate it? 10 being amazing. 1 being complete misery."

"6.5. So it wasn't horrible at all," Debby answers honestly. "But...here is how I think about it now. This is what I tell clients, and I ask clients that same question. I believe, firmly, when someone answers that question with anything below an 8, he or she needs to change jobs. And here's why..."

"Seriously?" Steven interrupts.

"Yeah, I do."

"Is it only you that thinks that?"

"Probably," Debby chuckles. "This is how I think about it. If you are below an 8, think about when you were in school, what is a 75?"

"C. Average," Steven responds immediately, his number one core value centering on excellence.

"You spend the bulk of your waking life at your job. Do you want the bulk of your waking life to be average? Or below average? And I'll get on my soapbox for a minute, those of us that have the education and the ability..."

Steven cuts Debby short, his body covered in chills. "Wait. How many times have you said that to someone? Over 100?"

"No, because it has just crystallized for me over the last year. But I am really clear about it now. How does that sit with you, by the way?"

"Me?"

"Yeah, you."

"I got goose bumps."

"Did you?"

"Yeah."

"So, I got something?" A broad, bright smile spreads across Debby's face.

"Yeah. You got something." Steven's mind drifts far away from their conversation.

"Good. That's going in my book, too!" Debby exclaims.

"It's huge. I would say a 6.5 is pretty good, but after you explained it…."

"It occurred to me as I was talking to people. What I am driving at is, if you have the means and the education to make a change, you have an obligation to make the change. I believe we have an obligation to change."

"An obligation to whom?"

"To the world, the universe, to God—for me it's God—I think about it this way…"

"So is this getting to our purpose, one's meaning?"

"Maybe. Let me get these thoughts out…"

Steven scrawls frantically. "Did you say a *responsibility* to change?"

"I said an obligation."

"Because you are not—because we are not—doing what we are meant to be doing?" Steven scrambles to attain clarity.

"Because, OK—I am going to get all 'woo-woo' now—energetically when we feel less fulfilled, less happy, when we are contributing less than what we could be and want to be…of course, we could all always be doing more, but coaching for me is where I vibrate at the highest frequency. The world needs me to do that so I can contribute to the greater expansion of everything else."

Steven knew there was a reason he clicked so well with Debby. They hold the same beliefs about one's purpose, about one's life's meaning.

"For me, what I found is, I am having the biggest impact I am capable of having when I am being an executive coach. Are you getting too much?" Debby finishes her train of thought.

"No. No. No. I am just sitting here realizing that some of the exact same things that drive you are the things that drive me. I know I am here on this planet to inspire people to be better people. And I am willing to roll up my sleeves and get my hands dirty. It is what I am supposed to do. It makes me happy."

Steven re-directs the interview. "So let's change gears a little bit. How many professionals have you coached?"

Debby thinks for a second. "Ballpark...250."

"What is the range of salaries of people you have coached?"

"Five figures up to tens of millions."

Steven pauses for a moment. "Switching gears again...how do you stay thin?"

Debby laughs as if she weren't expecting that question. "I exercise six days a week."

"For how long?"

"Anywhere from thirty minutes to one and a half hours."

"How long have you exercised for six days a week for thirty to ninety minutes?"

"Almost two years."

"Only two years? You weren't chubby before?"

"No. I was never chubby. I have exercised in fits and spurts for most of my adult life. I drink a lot of water. I am a vegetarian."

"Are you aware of the calories you eat?"

"Yes absolutely, and I don't completely restrict any food."

"Do you think about your weight?"

"Yes," Debby admits.

"Do you want to be thin?"

"Yes."

"Are you doing what you were meant to do?"

"Well, philosophical conversation for a minute: I don't think that each of us only has one thing that we were meant to do. You often hear of the person who always knew they wanted to be a surgeon or a nurse or a school teacher. Those people aside—they are a small percentage of the population.

"For most of us, I think there are lots of things that we can do and that we would do well…We may find one thing and stick with it, and we could as easily have found another one that we would have been equally good at and equally passionate about."

"Do you have dreams? Do you mind sharing them if you do?"

"Well one dream of mine is to be a published author and to speak frequently on my book, or books. I envision myself as a keynote speaker. And if I could snap my fingers and do anything I wanted to do, I would probably be the next Oprah. I love the idea of having my own talk show."

Steven quickly looks up from his Livescribe. "Really? I didn't know that. Why didn't you ever tell me that? You and I have the same exact dream."

"Well, maybe we could have a 'He Said, She Said' of sorts?"

"I don't know, maybe. Interesting...What did you think when I was telling you that was my dream?"

"Well, I am not allowed to say, 'Yeah, me too!'" Debby responds sarcastically. "That's why I am helping you with your book. If you said your dream was to go out and dig up a patch of grass, I would have said great, and I would have looked into my rolodex to find someone to help you dig up the grass. But I wouldn't be holding a shovel there with you." Debby explains matter-of-factly.

"So I want your opinion on certain things. What are three non-tangible things that will determine if a particular individual will be able to change careers?"

Debby thinks for a moment as she looks through her notes, "I was expecting that question...Give me a second."

Debby finds her list of non-tangibles. "**Determination.** Determined to make a change. Someone could be really unhappy but really unwilling to do anything about it, someone with a stuck mentality."

"OK. That makes sense."

"**Willingness to network and talk to people.** People who are most successful changing careers do informational interviews; they strengthen their networks to find people who can help them step into their next career path; it is always through people that the next opportunity is created.

"**Clarity and openness.** Be as clear as you can be and be absolutely open to whatever might show up. When you start the process, you are telling the universe to let things flow toward you. The clarity of the intention is what attracts these opportunities to you. You just have to listen."

Steven stares past Debby, thinking about how he met Amelia at the coffee machine that day. Amelia appeared immediately after Steven became clear as to what he was writing his first book about. Steven tunes back in and keeps going with his interview questions. "Does every person have a different formula for success depending on how they rate their core values?"

"Yes, I believe so."

"So every individual's measure of success is unique?"

"Yes."

"Ummmm...The people you have successfully helped through coaching, is part of what you do bringing people in alignment with their core values?"

"Yes, absolutely that is what I do, and a lot of times people don't even know that they have core values."

"So you are raising their level of awareness?"

"We are in a society that teaches people that success is the next job, the next car, the next material thing. All of those things may be goals, but once you attain them you check the box."

"Living life in concert with one's core values is what determines an individual's success in life?"

"Yes. I would wholeheartedly agree with that."

"OK. So does that mean someone cannot be successful if they do not understand what their core values are?"

"It means that that person cannot *feel* successful. They may look successful to the outside world, but they will not experience success for themselves."

"Do you think a person's destiny is to reach a place where they are living a life that is in concert with their true values and they are vibrating at the highest frequency they can at any given moment?"

Debby considers Steven's questions for a moment. "I would say, a person's destiny is to be living a full, evenly-balanced life and they are fully engaged in the process of that life, living in the moment, even when the moment sucks."

"Debby, I think this is a good stopping point. Thank you so much for your time! Can we meet again to finish up the questions I have for you?" Steven asks politely as he smiles and walks Debby to her car.

"Sure. I'll send you some dates that will work for me.

Steven watches Debby's blue Volvo drive away. He stares for an eternity through the trees at the end of the parking lot hundreds of yards away, long after her car is long gone.

I am becoming an author, Steven thinks to himself. *I am becoming an author.*

Chapter 22
Be True to Yourself

Debby Stone Interview Part 2:
Work within your natural abilities

Steven flips through his notebook as he greets Debby at the Starbucks on Mansell Road.

"I know we're pressed for time so let's jump right in...Last time I asked you if there are traits that pre-dispose someone for career success and you said: 'Knowing yourself. Taking ownership and making conscious choices. The ability to authentically self-promote. Being effective at building and maintaining relationships. Working within your natural abilities.'" Steven immediately starts the interview so they will not be rushed.

"Yep. I remember."

"Can you elaborate on these?"

"Sure, I made some notes...Let's see...being true to yourself, what do I mean by that....

"Being true to yourself involves being aware of where you are strong and where your limitations are so that you can surround yourself, perhaps, with people who are strong where you are not. Being true to yourself means operating in a way that suits you—picking a path that suits your values, your goals, your abilities, and your skills. Take the path that is really a fit for who you are, and of course, you will not know what path that is without knowing yourself. So get to know yourself!

"**Taking ownership and making conscious choices**. For many of us, we fall into career paths, and what I find in coaching is that people get to some point—whether it's 28, 38, 45, or 50 years old—and they realize they have had a fair amount of career success, but it's just happened, there was no conscious path. For you to ultimately be successful, at some point, you have to take the reins and not just wait for someone to go, 'hey you might be great for this role, would you like it?' Rather than passively accepting what comes your way, you need to consciously think about what kind of role would suit you, and then try to create the opportunity you would want rather than passively waiting and being reactive."

"OK. So active versus passive." Steven jots down the word *active*.

"**The ability to authentically self-promote**. I always recommend my clients read the book, *Brag: The Art of Tooting Your Own Horn without Blowing It*. The ability to self-promote is critical because, in today's world, if you don't tell people what you bring to the table and how you do what it is that you do, they are not simply going to notice, at least not in a way that correlates to what you have achieved. People are moving too fast, there is too much information, and you have to be able to tell your story if you want to be successful in the way and in the role that you want. So the ability to self-promote, and do it in a way that is authentic and not over the top, is an important success factor."

"OK. Got it."

"**Being effective at building relationships and networking**. Really what this means is that *people* are the backbone of any career path, whether you are collaborating with people, trying to enroll people in your vision, or manage a team. In order to be successful, you have to be able to build relationships. Very few people can be successful as an island...Especially if you are making a career change. The people who really work their networks, those people are able to find new jobs. They are able to forge new paths. People who sit at home and try to use the Internet to find their next job really do not have a lot of success. Blindly sending résumés or cold calling people really isn't the way that jobs are found these days. It's all about the relationships."

"OK. Got it. Makes sense."

"Working within your natural abilities. "We are all hardwired to do certain things naturally and easily. We can learn to do other things that are not within our natural wheelhouse, but we will never be as good at them. When we are operating within our natural abilities, we are able to contribute more, feel more fulfilled, and things are just plain easier. It's that comfort of ease." Debby pauses for a moment to think of a good example.

"For example, I could learn how to build a car engine, because I am not a dumb person; however, it is so far outside of my natural wheelhouse that every step of it would be painful."

"So, you're not going to help me dig a ditch or learn to be a mechanic any time soon?" Steven asks sarcastically.

"No, probably not anytime soon." Debby smiles and chuckles at Steven's sarcasm.

"Now let's change direction and focus on advice about changing careers." Steven transitions into the next area of questions for Debby.

"Do you have specific techniques you use to help someone change careers?"

"Yes...I'm trying to think how to say this somewhat succinctly. Give me a second." Rather than look up or away, Debby just focuses even more intently on Steven as she searches for what she wants to say. "A couple of things are important. First is what I said before, getting to know yourself, so I help my clients get to know their values, their goals, their skills, their abilities, their passions, and their interests. And then we also look at what they like and dislike in the work world based on their experience. So overall, my technique is to take those things and combine them, and what we usually find is, if we mush all of that together, certain career paths are indicated.

"I also have them think way outside of the box in terms of fantasy careers, dream jobs, if you will, so they have the opportunity to dream big and discover what it is that attracts them to certain professions."

"Can you give me an example?" Steven inches forward ever-so-slightly in his seat.

"If someone says their dream job is to be a neurosurgeon and I know they don't want to spend $200,000 to go back to school, I would ask them to tell me what it is about this specialty that interests them. Is it the level of detail? Is it working with the brain? Is it taking care of patients? Is it working with your hands? What is it about that career that attracts you to it that can be incorporated into your current career transition?"

"OK. Makes a lot of sense."

"Then I can bring the conversation with a client back to what she can practically do."

"So part of it is tactical like listing out things you like, dislike, your interests and part of it is dreaming or imagining?"

"Yes. Absolutely. This combination of the two helps to narrow it down."

"OK. So what do you do next after you do this inventory of the things that make a person tick?"

"OK. So let's use this one guy I worked with as an example. He had two options after going through this process: (1) open up a photography business; (2) teach school."

"Wow! Very different." Steven loves listening to Debby talking about her passion.

"So he had these two options and both seemed relatively equal, but one hit more of his core values than the other. Long story short, he ended up opening a photography business because one of his core values was around creativity. He is doing great with it, too. Before you decide upon a course of action, you make a map of both different outcomes. In this case, opening up a photography business or being a school teacher and you see which one has a greater chance of turning out better. And which one, as you get closer and closer to it, feels more and more like the right choice."

"It's interesting; I interviewed Amelia and she did all of the things you have mentioned, but kind of made up the process on her own."

"Good girl!" Debby exclaims enthusiastically. "I like to have people explore two or three paths at the same time; it's more time efficient. I recommend you do a lot of interviewing and lots of reading. I have had people do volunteer vacations where they try out a job. Whatever we can do to get them as close as they can be to trying it out."

"What's a volunteer vacation?" Steven tilts his head to the side slightly and squints his left eye.

"There are places where you can sign on...you pay money, and you get to go and be an apprentice chef in a restaurant for a week. And you work. You work sixty hours in a week to see if the career is something that you would enjoy. But you're paying. It's your vacation. Or you get to work at a bed and breakfast and see what it is really like..."

"That's awesome!" Steven chimes in. "Do you have some list of all of the different careers in the world?"

"Nope, but there are career counselors who do and there are books that do, but what I find typically is that people know what they are attracted to. If we have someone who gets really stumped, we have a couple of things we typically do. We may have them ask people in their world, what their friends/acquaintances see them doing?"

"OK. Amelia did that too!" *No wonder Amelia did such a great job changing careers. She did everything right.*

"Or, I may send them to Barnes & Noble and have them wander around and ask them to notice what types of books they are most attracted to. What are the subjects that they are interested in, and then we explore what careers are related to those subjects. If you are constantly picking up landscape gardening, that says something, maybe there is a passion there."

"That's how I decided to go to graduate school and get my master's in counseling psychology. Every time I went to the bookstore, I was in the self-help section; I loved reading about psychology and personal improvement."

"Interesting. See? It's good advice," Debby chuckles.

Steven scans down his list of questions and moves on. "How can people determine if they are doing what they are meant to do with their lives? Do people have a 'purpose'?"

"I don't believe that most people have a calling."

"You don't? Are you sure?"

Debby responds emphatically, "I do not. I think there are a few people who do, but this is a small minority. Of course, you have the young child that will say, 'I knew since I was six I wanted to be a surgeon when my daddy had this operation.' Or, 'I always played the role of the teacher when we were kids and played school, so I knew I wanted to be a teacher.'

"But, in general, for most of us, there are a number of different careers that we can have that will make us happy. And I also believe most of us will all have multiple careers in our lives. Very few of us will start and end in the same career. A career that fulfills us in our twenties may not when we are in our thirties or forties. Or when we are forty-five," Debby emphasizes the word "forty-five" and gives Steven a little wink.

"So...what I heard you say, but you didn't say it, is that as our values change, our careers may need to change too?"

"I wouldn't say values. Values are stable. So who you are does not change. But what your goals are and what your life is like changes. So for example, when you are twenty-five and you don't have any roots and you want to see the world, a job that allows you to travel three to four days per week or move around a lot may be perfect for you. However, when you are forty, you are married, you have 2.2 kids and suddenly you don't want to be gone three to four days per week; you don't want to live far away from your aging parents. There are priorities that shift." Debby continues, an emphatic confidence oozing from her voice. "I actually believe for many of us, we get tired of doing something. So it may be that a career shift is necessary because you have been at a job for seven, ten, fifteen years and you are ready for something different."

Steven interjects, summarizing what he has heard as he learned how to do in *The Art of Helping* class he took so many years ago. "From a certain perspective, if a person gets in touch with their values, their skills, and what they enjoy and transitions from accepting life passively to actively going after what it is that will make them happy, we can advocate changing careers with confidence?"

"Yes. Absolutely. I always say, we can find the *right career* for you *right now*, but I will not guarantee that this is what you will be doing the day that you retire," Debby pauses. "I want to say one more thing before we move on. I think there are a lot of things one can do to fulfill their life's purpose. I don't believe that career and purpose are the same thing. Purpose might be to help people learn, but there are lots and lots of ways that you can have an influence on helping people to learn. Someone's purpose may be to help people to heal. They may be a doctor, a nurse, a physical therapist, a counselor, or a massage therapist. There are many different permutations that exist."

"So you do believe that people have a 'purpose'?"

"I believe that people have a purpose, *broadly defined*. I think broadly defined we all have something that lights us up."

"So...I guess you answered this next question, too...." Steven chuckles as he reads through his list of questions, determined to ask all of the questions his book advisor says are "excellent." "Does someone need to earn his living in service to his purpose?"

"It is ideal if you can implement your purpose through your work, because you spend the bulk of your waking hours at work. If you don't feel fulfilled at work, you better be getting it somewhere else, or you are going to be a mighty unhappy individual. So if your purpose is to help people heal, and your day job is an accountant, then you would probably want to be volunteering at something like a rape crisis center, for example, so that you are honoring that aspect of who you are."

Steven thinks about this for a moment. "What if an accountant makes $90,000 per year and it provides a stable income for his family, and he makes the choice to sacrifice his desire to help people to be a good provider for his family?"

"Yep. And he may enjoy it BECAUSE he is honoring a core value of family or responsibility or stability, perhaps. But if there is some part of his purpose that is not being fulfilled, he will have to get that outside of work. When we don't get all of our values met at work, in order to avoid feeling very unhappy, we have to get these values met somewhere else," Debby pauses for a moment and repositions herself. "Let's say someone has a core value around being creative, and for whatever reason they have no creativity in their job, they are definitely going to want to be painting in the evening, or writing, or taking a sculpting class."

"Gotcha…So let's say all things being equal, of course a 45-year-old person without a college degree isn't going to be a neurosurgeon, but let's say an accountant changing to a real estate agent, or a teacher changing to a graphic designer, what is a realistic timeframe someone should have in his mind to make this kind of change?"

"Six to twelve months. That is generally realistic. I have had people make shifts faster, and I have had people make changes more slowly."

"So someone who is forty or forty-five, kids all in school, has a college degree, maybe their résumé is eight to ten years old, how do they get experience in a new role when they have been out of the workforce for so long?" Steven thinks about Michele as he asks this question.

"OK. The first thing they can do is volunteer. Let's say it's the former teacher who wants to be the graphic artist; she can volunteer to be on the PTA and be in charge of the newsletter, or do graphics for the newsletter, or the posters that need to be made for some function. Volunteering gives them the opportunity to learn, and the experience they gain is real and can be put on a résumé.

"The second thing is to take classes wherever possible. If you want to be that graphic artist, take classes in Photoshop or some other graphics program. The other thing I recommend is that you work, one to two days a week, with someone who does this for a living, sort of as an apprenticeship."

Steven interjects, calling upon his experience from when he ran a small consulting company. "That's the number one advice I would give: volunteer to work for a small company that does what it is you want to do to gain the experience."

"Yup. You're essentially an intern at that point."

"The corporate recruiters I have spoken to have given this advice as well. When I was a small business owner, if I had someone come in and they are working extremely hard, you are not going to let that person work for free. You will figure out some way to pay that person."

"No, most people wouldn't," Debby changes the inflection of her voice slightly. "At least not forever. You are either going to help that person find a job, or you are going to hire them, or pay them a reduced wage."

"By following this internship route, they would be getting the experience in their new field of interest. Of course, they would be networking at the same time, telling their friends of their new career choice, joining professional organizations...."

"Yes, absolutely."

"So is the reason that people can't change jobs is that they are unwilling to put one foot in front of the other and do these simple things you mention? Or that they are too proud to take an unpaid internship?"

"Yes, that is some of it, but there may be practical limitations that exist for some people that do not exist for other people. But yes, for the most part, you are correct. People are unwilling to work as hard as they might need to."

Steven really wants to make sure Debby was saying what he truly believed. "So is it as easy as flipping a switch in your mind and saying I am going to do this, no matter how hard it is?"

Debby ponders this question for a second. "Yes, in a certain way it is. We all know people who are victims of this or victims of that and they will never be able to make a change because they do not take accountability for their actions."

Wanting to be respectful of Debby's time, Steven says, "OK. We have five more minutes. What advice would you give someone who is changing careers?"

"First thing that pops into my mind is to be patient. It's a process; it's not a snap your fingers and it appears kind of thing."

"Do they need a coach, some kind of…ummm…uhhh…partner?" Steven struggles to ask the question, determined not to use the term, "accountability partner." Steven hates corporate jargon, catch phrases, and overused buzzwords.

"It's a good question. I think accountability always helps, so whether it is a coach, or a buddy, or someone who is interested in changing careers that you know, and you meet for breakfast once a week, or you're a part of a career transition group at church." Debby pauses for a moment. "I don't think you have to have a coach, but I do think that you have to have a plan."

"OK. OK. Thank you so much." *You heard it all here first folks. Special thanks to Debby Stone. Debby is someone whose life is working, she exercises regularly and consistently, she has control of her diet and she loves what she is doing (most days).*

Chapter 23
Today Doesn't Begin Today. It Begins Yesterday.

One Sunday, Steven re-reads the "Today Doesn't Begin Today. It Begins Yesterday." chapter and spends the weekend totally depressed.

The chapter basically sucks. Are things presented out of order? Has he slapped disjointed, half-baked thoughts onto the page, jumping from one idea to the next because he is lazy, not investing the requisite time to construct a well-thought-out chapter? Or is it like his Naysayer would say, "I don't want to read a fucking book about you fucking mentoring someone."

Or is it all of these things?

The fact that someone asked you to mentor her shows the changes you are making are showing up in the world, Steven counters his Naysayer's voice, wondering if it will always exist. *Go get your dirty workout clothes out of the trunk of your car, Steven. It's Sunday. Bring your gym bag upstairs so you can pack it for the week. Baby steps, Steven. Baby steps.* Steven attempts to coax himself out of his depression at 10:00 a.m. on Sunday morning and figure out what to do with this train wreck of a chapter.

Now, write in your food journal for Friday night, all day Saturday and Sunday morning. Steven continues coaching himself. *Do the easy things you know you can do.*

Steven takes out his food journal. Between Friday night and Sunday late morning he has consumed: two Texas Margaritas; one glass of Chardonnay; two pieces of pizza; an Asiago bagel with turkey sausage, cheddar cheese and egg; and other stuff his size zero trainer, Julie, will have a field day with. *No wonder I have only lost four pounds in the last three months*, Steven thinks to himself as an email indicator appears on his phone.

Aara Parkour, a woman Steven occasionally works with at his company, emails. Steven scans her email and a strange, thoughtful expression shows up on his face.

From: Aara Parkour
To: Steven Sharp
Subject: Mentoring

Steven,

I have been meaning to send this email since we had our last CWN meeting [CWN stands for *{Company Name} Women's Network*...don't even ask why Steven was at the CWN meeting] and you talked about your values that you developed as part of the mentoring or coaching you have been having. You talked about what you had to do to prioritize how much tennis you were playing based on your values....

I was impressed by what you were saying, and I was wondering if you would be a mentor for me where you teach me what you are learning from your personal coaching?

Please do not feel any pressure – let me know your thoughts? I was thinking we can have lunch and chat – this is an overdue lunch that I actually wanted to schedule since the first project we worked on together ☺

Aara Parkour
Marketing

Steven stares into space as he clicks "Reply." *Someone actually listened to what I had to say.*

From: Steven Sharp
To: Aara Parkour
Subject: Re: Mentoring

Hi Aara,

What a great email! When I shared at CWN, I didn't think what I was saying really resonated with anyone. So I was kind of surprised (in a pleasant way) to get your email this evening.

Anyways, I'd be honored to mentor you. I think it would be a great experience for both of us, as you mentioned.

Let's grab a cup of coffee (easier than lunch) and figure out what the mentoring relationship could look like.

Thank you for thinking of me. I am really flattered, Aara.

Steven

Almost immediately, Steven receives a response from Aara, even though it is Sunday.

From: Aara Parkour
To: Steven Sharp
Subject: RE: Mentoring

Good morning – I am glad to hear of your thoughts and reaction......

I was listening ☺ I am honored.

I will put something on our calendars – not sure if you like to get coffee here and sit in the university or go to Starbucks for a coffee break?

Aara

On June 19, 2013, Steven and Aara meet for their first meeting. During the course of the session, Aara confesses, "I know I need to dress differently, but I am lazy in the morning. I go into my closet and I can't find anything I want to wear that doesn't make me look fat." Aara pauses. "So I throw on anything—a pair of jeans and sloppy top or I work from home."

"I thought I was the only one who struggled with getting out of bed in the morning and getting dressed for work. Mornings are tough, aren't they?"

"For me they are," Aara admits. "I'd really like to be perceived as more of a leader. I feel professional inside, just not showing it externally. I see 'So and So' during a panel discussion talking about ways to organize your time and ways to prioritize, and I think to myself *I can do that*."

Steven falls silent for a minute, and he has stopped nodding his head like he had learned how to do in graduate school to let someone know he was listening. Steven stares over Aara's head at the messy whiteboard behind her as he figures out how to ask the next question. "You realize what you have told me today?"

"No, I am not sure that I do."

"You began this session telling me that you wanted to dress better—to have the external you match the internal you—but that you are 'too lazy' in the morning to dress professionally."

"Yes. I did tell you that," Aara begrudgingly admits.

"Have you thought about going into your closet to select a professional outfit the night before so you don't have to decide in the morning?"

Aara smiles sheepishly. "Yes, I've heard that before."

"Well, why don't you do it? Make a commitment that you will go into your closet tonight and pick out something professional so you don't have to make the decision in the morning. Today doesn't begin today, Aara. It begins yesterday."

Aara pauses for a moment to think about this, "OK, I'll do it." She grins, the gold tones of her olive skin light up, and her freckles seem to pop even more.

"Next time we get together, we need to set some goals for our time together," Steven says to Aara as they walk out of the conference room together and Steven turns off the fluorescent light.

 As Steven writes, he listens to his *Steven Typical Playlist* as "The Promise" by Tracy Chapman floods his ear buds. The lyrics, "If you wait for me, then I'll come for you," make him consider this person he is becoming has been waiting for him for a very long time.

Today doesn't begin today, Steven thinks to himself as he *writes* his narrative nonfiction rather than typing some disjointed prose into one of his Apple mobile devices or scribbling in his Livescribe® notebook. *You can't have the day you want to have, unless it is preceded by a night that prepares you for the day you want to have. Your day begins not when you are putting on an outfit that looks ridiculous, but when you neglected to realize you had nothing clean you wanted to wear the night before. Your day begins when you don't pack your workout clothes in the car the night before so that you can work out on your lunch hour. Your day begins when you have nothing to bring to the office for a healthy lunch. In so many ways, today doesn't begin today; it begins yesterday.*

Next, Steven looks at his "Morning Ritual" recurring appointments he had set for himself all of those months ago that supported the person he wanted to become. In order to follow a morning ritual, first you must have one. Ask yourself: What makes you feel more awake in the morning and what makes you feel more asleep? And then do the things that make you feel more awake. Am I neurotic? No, just getting into a good routine and establishing healthy habits.

What makes you start your day with confidence and what makes you start your day with apprehension? Do the things that make you start your day with confidence.

Steven stops working on his book for a moment and sends a text to Julie.

I am on my ninth day in a row of my food journal!!!!!

Awesome! Proud of you!
When do I get to see it?

Soon, Steven thinks. Soon.

I am almost ready. You'll be the first to know☺

Chapter 24
It Has to Come from Within

Wednesday, 6:45 a.m.
Starbucks on Peachtree and 7th ST

"Hi Bonnie. It's been so long!!" Steven exclaims. "You know...I read the whole thing last night, and, and...ummmm. It's getting there."

"It is. It's getting there. When writing, you have to strike a balance so that you don't bore your more sophisticated reader and you don't lose a reader who is new to your subject matter. Make sense?"

"Yes. It does. I am starting to see that women have a very different professional experience than men do. Women's career decisions differ greatly from how men make their career decisions."

"In what ways? You mean like all of the externalities?"

Damn she is smart.

Bonnie reads the look on his face and continues, "I just went to this conference where they said men were very good at stopping a task if it didn't immediately align with their purpose. While with women, they will tend to prolong it, delay, make excuses...."

Just like Amelia did with her Ph.D. program.

"OK. Let's keep going. Has Stephanie come back from Haiti yet? What about Amelia? Is she going to let you tell about her externalities that influenced her?"

"Yes. Stephanie is back; she only went for a week. She has returned…Is that whole trip to Haiti something that fits into this book?"

"You know, it could fit in multiple places. Ultimately, does the country of Haiti really want to change for itself? It has to, has to, has to come from within. Haiti becomes a microcosm of the things you are trying to say. It has been this way for 40 years; it has all of these externalities pressing upon it—terrible political corruption, massive diseases, hurricanes—ultimately, the country has to heal from within."

"Got it. So it fits?"

"Yes, it fits. It would be great if you could get Stephanie to write something like that, about the externalities and how so many things are outside of its control. And it will come out, because that is the way that it is in Haiti."

"OK. Not sure about Amelia yet…So what do I do about Michele? She is caught up with raising her family. Now her son, Daniel, is having problems in school and Michele is taking him from one specialist to another. I feel like I am one more thing she has to worry about."

"Let's think about it, OK?"

"OK. I am really starting to get inspired by my book!" Steven admits with a mounting sense of pride.

"That needs to go in your closing. One of the main things I wrote in this iteration of your book when I was taking notes: 'promises to the reader.' You have to think about the promises that you make to the reader and you have to fulfill the promises that you make to your reader. You can never ever leave the reader hanging. You have to delight and satisfy your reader."

"OK. I will work on it," Steven promises as he packs up to head to the office. When he arrives at work, he bumps into Amelia in the parking deck.

"Good morning! How are you?" Amelia greets Steven, her smile showing a little bit of thoughtfulness.

"I'm great...Just came from meeting with my book advisor."

"I have been thinking about what you asked me to think about, and I am OK with you sharing the personal things we discussed during my interview as to why I ended up in the wrong career path."

"Thank you, Amelia. And let's change your name so you feel comfortable with what gets included. I think what you shared will be tremendously helpful for others to read."

Steven hunts down the transcript of the interview he conducted with Amelia so many months ago. He edits it to shorten it and includes the essence of it here.

"So when you were a little girl, did you know what you wanted to do when you grew up?"

"I thought I wanted to be a doctor," Amelia answers honestly.

"A medical doctor?"

"Yes, a medical doctor. But I don't know if I thought I wanted to be a doctor, or my dad wanted me to be a doctor. And society wanted me to be a doctor."

"Your dad? Society? What does that mean?"

"My dad was a physician and every one in his extended family is a physician, an attorney, a dentist, a psychologist. Everyone there has some kind of secondary degree because schooling was free in Argentina where he was raised."

"When did you first challenge in your own mind that you didn't want to be a doctor?"

"My freshman year in college when I said to my father: 'I don't want to be a doctor.'"

Both Steven and Amelia laugh loudly.

"That was a really big deal because I had never stood up to him before in my life. In retrospect, I knew I liked the field of psychology; I was willing to pursue a Ph.D. as an 'olive branch' of sorts for disappointing him for not pursuing my M.D.," Amelia stares past Steven, her mouth no longer turned up at the corners.

"I began to do poorly in chemistry and I started to think: Am I doing this for my father? Or am I doing this because this is what I truly wanted to do?"

"Were there any pipe dreams when you were a little girl that you would be anything other than a doctor?" Steven wonders aloud.

Amelia responds immediately, "Yes, a fashion designer!"

"Is that still inside of you somewhere?"

"Yeah, the creative side of me still is. My mom was very for it, she said do whatever you want to do and my dad was not as supportive." Amelia changes her tone and expression to be more direct like her father. "'That's not a real career, why would you want to do that? You would be a phenomenal doctor. You're a woman; you are really good at math and science. There are not that many women in the field. You could go to Georgia Tech, get an engineering degree and then go to medical school.'"

"So you tell your dad you didn't want to be a medical doctor... How did you end up in a Ph.D. program in clinical psychology?"

"After I got my undergraduate degree in psychology, I took a job with an organization that does stuff with developmentally-handicapped children. I did that and studied for my GRE."

"When you did that, did any part of you question your motives? Or is that what propelled you forward and moved you toward getting your doctorate degree in clinical psychology?"

"Both. I say both because I knew I did not want to work with severely developmentally-handicapped individuals for the rest of my life. I wanted to be a therapist with higher functioning individuals who were dealing with more internalizing disorders: generalized anxiety disorder, depression, OCD, et cetera."

"Got it. OK. How far were you into the doctorate program when you had your 'existential epiphany' you mentioned to me at the coffee machine that day?"

Amelia chuckles. "About four years...When I was in graduate school I knew that I had three options: (1) being a therapist; (2) being a researcher; or (3) being an academic, and usually if you are an academic you have to publish or perish. I realized I didn't love any one of them to make a full forty-hour work week. And, I definitely did not want to be a researcher the rest of my life. I didn't want to submit to the pressure of having to publish or perish in my first five years."

"So none of these things was like, I can't wait to wake up on Monday morning and listen to people's problems or do research or...."

"Right. None of them was exciting to me. So I started to plan out the things I would need to do to graduate: my comp's paper, writing a grant to propose for my dissertation, and I also needed to do my externship after I finished my program because I was done with all of my classes. So I had another year or so left, I would say, before I would have been completely done," Amelia pauses for moment. "I started to plan things out, and there was this...there was this immense dread that came over me whenever I started to think about the things I still had to do to finish my program. So one day, I spent an hour or two at Starbucks thinking about things, and I started to think: am I having this tremendous dread because this is not going to be easy, or am I having this tremendous dread because this isn't going to be easy because I am absolutely miserable in what I am doing, and I don't foresee myself really going anywhere once I have done this?"

Amelia goes on. "It's one thing to be at a point in your career and you realize this is the long haul and it's time to jump in. It's scary to know the next year is going to be really insanely long hours and no sleep. That's one thing. That's one kind of dread, one way to be overwhelmed. But, would you submit to that level of being overwhelmed if you knew in the back of your mind that you were not really going to be happy when you were done anyway?"

"So when you asked yourself that question at Starbucks, did you get an immediate answer like, 'no I'm feeling overwhelmed because this is not what I want to do'?"

"No, I didn't get an immediate answer at Starbucks. About three or four weeks later I literally woke up in a cold sweat one night. I was home on a sabbatical from the program to help my mom who wasn't doing well. I must have had a dream or something; I don't know; I don't really remember the dream; it was something that shook me to the core. I lay in bed wide awake for the rest of the night, and I realized I cannot do this. This is not for me," Amelia pauses for a second and takes a few cleansing breaths.

"So what did you do with that realization? You have a master's degree in this field, you have four years of your life invested in your doctorate, and your dad has always thought that you would be a doctor, what goes on inside a person?"

"You know, it's funny you mention my father; I think a big part of it for me was pressure from my father, and the other part of it was societal. You know I have always been so structured and so by the books: I was a straight A-student in school, I always played by the rules, I always did exactly what I was supposed to do, I never got in trouble, and I was valedictorian of my high school. You know, what do you do with that?" Amelia's voice trails off for a brief moment. "You go off to a really great school; you get a professional degree. I mean there are all of these pressures around that. Nobody says, 'ok you're a valedictorian, go and be a clothes designer,' which is what I wanted to do, but it doesn't have the prestige of saying 'I'm a doctor.' Does that make sense?"

"Oh. I hear what you're saying."

"I don't even know where I was going with all of that," Amelia admits, her still strong emotions taking her mind on a journey she could neither control nor influence.

Steven restates the question for Amelia, "The question was, you have a master's in your field and almost a doctorate and you realize this career path is not right for you. What goes on inside of that person at that time when you come to that realization?"

"You know I think part of it was a pride thing for me because there were expectations from high school, ya know. People assumed that I was going to be the most successful one that graduated. I also had that peer-level pressure, and then I also had that pressure from my father. The interesting thing...you know, the thing that ultimately released me?"

Steven thinks for a second to see if he can guess where Amelia's release came from. "No. What ultimately released you?"

"I went to dinner one night with my dad, in the car he started to ask me, 'Are you getting ready to go back to Nebraska, do you have everything planned, do you need help?' And I just started crying. And I cried during the entire dinner...I told him how unhappy I was, and I didn't want to go back; I wasn't looking forward to it. That I didn't want to be a doctor; I hadn't been happy for a long time, and I wasn't happy with my career choice. I wasn't happy being in Nebraska. I wasn't happy being away from my friends and family. I wasn't happy with any of it." Amelia stops recounting from memory and addresses Steven directly. "Steven, it wasn't just my career choice, but that I felt so isolated and so alone; I was away from everybody that I loved."

"I understand," Steven sympathizes.

"At that dinner my dad said to me, 'If you're not happy, come home.'" Amelia's voice softens as she remembers this grant of permission from her father, deep rooted in love. "So all this time I was putting all this pressure on myself based on what he wanted, and he was like, 'I have missed you for the last four years, come home.' I invested four years of my life pursuing a career based on what I thought my father could accept from me, and I was wrong. All he wanted for me was to be happy. That's all I think he has ever wanted." Amelia's voice cracks a little as her eyes swell with tears.

"So what I am really hearing you say is that in our lives we have responsibilities and loyalties to others, but we also have responsibilities and loyalties to ourselves. Looking back, would you have done anything differently?"

Amelia stares at Steven and he stares back; three different people walk past the conference room where they are meeting. Finally, Amelia answers, "I don't know. I really was just miserable the whole time anyway, so I don't know. I can't really answer that question.

"I love psychology and I still wanted to please my father, even at the expense of pleasing myself. I just don't know."

"Fair enough. OK. I totally get all of that. Thank you for opening up and sharing all of that with me. I think anyone who reads this book will find your story incredibly helpful."

As Steven thanks Amelia one last time, his mind is elsewhere thinking about the ideas we hold that influence what we become.

What ideas do I hold that are influencing what I am to become? Who am I trying to please?

Chapter 25
Being Tired Doesn't Matter

Steven and Aara get together for their bi-monthly mentoring appointment. Steven opens the session with, "How are you? Do you have some written goals for us to discuss?"

"I am well. Yes, I spent some time with the goal setting worksheet you gave me. Are you ready?" Aara asks.

"Absolutely!" Steven responds.

"OK. You told me to think about five years from now and to think about the different dimensions of a healthy self...by the way, I love being able to think about my 'self' in terms of these different dimensions. It helps me to make sure I have balance in my life....

"My first goal: in five years, I would like to be a mother and have a four-year-old son or daughter. Second, I would like to have a job where I am paid what I am worth and that honors my core values. And third, I would like to be on the board of directors of a nonprofit organization that serves children or women in need."

"That is awesome!" Steven exclaims. "Those are great goals. Related to your goal of being a mother for the first time, do you mind if I ask how old you are?"

"I am forty-four." Aara's smile fades and her eyes fill with a slight sadness.

"I can see why you would want to start right away." Steven smiles at Aara as they both tear up slightly. Steven quickly changes the subject. "What does being on the board of directors of a nonprofit entail?"

"Primarily a time commitment and a financial commitment," Aara explains. Steven and Aara discuss her goals some more and the likelihood she will be able to conceive. They conclude their session with Aara agreeing to research adoption agencies at the same time she makes an appointment with a fertility specialist.

COACHING PREP FORM

How am I doing today?

> **Finally starting to lose some of the fat around my abdomen. What's changed? Keeping a food journal. I am on day 11. I have worked on my book a LOT this week. Forced myself to write every night – being tired doesn't matter.**

> **Proud of myself. Three days so far in the gym this week (out of three), by the time I see you it will be four. I am amazing. That was a joke☺ Can't wait to see you!**

What did I not get done that I intended to do?

> **WOW. I am not sure. Think I am humming along right now. Let me think about it.**

What are my current opportunities?

> **I need to start to market the idea of my book. I want to build out the website for my book. I want to start to use social media now.**

After working through his coaching prep form, he and Debby agree that he will complete his own goal setting worksheet.

First, I need to write the narrative of the person I want to be, Steven thinks. *I have to follow my own plan.* Steven envisions the person he wants to be and is immediately able to start writing about who that person is.

In March 2014, Steven Sharp attends his own book launch party for Forty-five is the New Twenty-five. *Leading up to that day, Meagan Gadreault has helped Steven establish a social media presence, and she is helping him get the idea of his book socialized. Cindy Lucas has built an amazing website for www.45isthenew25.com. Steven has gotten serious about his diet and consistent with his workouts. He has vowed to work out most days until his book launch. He has lost the last six to eight pounds of fat and weighs between 170 and 175 pounds. He runs at least two times per week. He has contacted all of TV's top talk show hosts, talk radio shows, bloggers, newspapers, and magazines announcing the arrival of* Forty-five is the New Twenty-five. *He has sent autographed, signed copies of his book and he follows everyone on Twitter. Anderson Cooper, Andy Cohen, Kris Jenner, Ellen DeGeneres, and Sanjay Gupta have all contacted Steven to suggest the possibility of him appearing on their talk shows to discuss the book.*

Steven loves his life, his book, his body, and is proud of what he has accomplished.

OK. Now I am ready to write down my goals. As Steven starts to identify his true goals, as opposed to untrue goals☺, he is fairly confident that the goals he starts to write down are real goals for him. He applies sort of a backward logic to arrive at this conclusion. Since the activities he is engaged in on a daily basis—his daily tasks, if you will— are working out each day, writing his book, and meeting with his book advisor, he is able to *infer* his longer term goals.

Steven's Long Term Goals

	1	2	3
Long Term Goals (3-5 years. Outcome based, results focused)	**Career/ Hobby** Have at least one book on the New York Times Best Seller List	**Regular Exercise** Have the body of an in-shape 25 y.o. Weigh 170 pounds and have a 32" or 33" waist	**Career** Be a Director or Senior Director of a Learning and Development Department
Interim Goals (1-2 years. Achievable, Outcome based)	Build book website	178 pounds; 34" waist	
	Have 10,000 followers on Twitter; Facebook page	Daily, regular, rigorous exercise part of my life.	
	Finish book; set to print; commission cover design	Run 2-3 times per week, MIN 5 miles	
	Outline complete for 48 is the New 28	Increased muscle mass. Body fat percentage <18%	
Short Term Goals/ Daily To Do Lists (3 months. Behavior based, not result focused)	Email Oprah, Ellen, Wendy Williams	Monday 1:00 p.m. Fit 360x	
		Tuesday Run	
		Wednesday 1:00 p.m. Fit 360x	
	Send press release to Atlanta media	Thursday, 1:1 w/JJ	
	Send press release to national media	Friday 6:40 a.m. group w/JJ	
	Build media contact database	Food journal daily	
	Write two blog posts per month and share	Fitbit® 10,000 steps/day	

Steven's Long Term Goals (Continued)

	4	**5**
Long Term Goals (3-5 years. Outcome based, results focused)	**Friendship/ Family of Choice** Have a close group of friends I love spending time with	**Financial** Be out of short term/ revolving credit card debt
Interim Goals (1-2 years. Achievable, Outcome based)	BE a friend to one person I admire. SHOW them I care; don't just care.	Pay off line of credit at bank
	BE a friend to another person I admire. SHOW them I care; don't just care.	Pay off American Express
Short Term Goals/ Daily To Do Lists (3 months. Behavior based, not result focused)	One time per month, do something with Jim's kids.	Spend one hour per day marketing book.
	One time per quarter, do something with Tina Sharp.	
	Talk to Bonnie about how I meet interesting people	
	Talk to my coach about how I meet interesting people	

Chapter 26
I Am Afraid…

Starbucks on Peachtree and 7th ST
6:45 a.m.

"We need to ratchet me back in the book," Bonnie opens the dialogue.

Steven sits there, stunned. "You are helping me to achieve this lifelong dream. It's important to me."

"OK. We can talk about it," Bonnie answers and switches gears. "You are using an action metaphor technique in this book, and I don't think you even know what that is."

"I don't! What is an action metaphor technique?" Steven asks excitedly, digging his pen into the lined notebook.

"With this technique, you actually act out what you are trying to teach. You don't just talk about it; you do it," Bonnie explains. "You are living the metaphor. You are living these principles you are stating will work. You are saying 'show me, don't tell me.' You give them a blank goal sheet and then you fill it in. It is more of an experiential approach than theoretical. The last section of this book needs to be called something like, 'Writing Your Own Book' or 'Telling Your Own Story.'"

Steven stares at Bonnie in complete amazement. His jaw falls to the floor and tears form in his eyes. *She understands what I am trying to do. She understands me*, Steven thinks, as he stretches across the table and high-fives a smiling Bonnie.

"We got this," Bonnie says confidently.

"This is going to be a powerful book!" Steven exclaims, as they high-five a second time. "I have an awesome team!" Steven pauses for a second, reveling in this journey he and Bonnie have been on together: A journey to being understood.

"You've got me; you've got my back on this, don't you?" Steven's voice breaks a little as the tears begin to overflow and stream down his face.

"Yes, I do," Bonnie confirms with a wide smile.

"I also wrote my first book club question. You know I have never been to a book club?"

"You haven't? You know, I go to one called BiblioBabes. Maybe I can see if they can make an exception for you?"

Steven cracks up, "What? I'm not a big enough babe for your book club that they would have to make an exception for me?" Bonnie and Steven laugh loudly, imagining Steven showing up at next month's BiblioBabes gathering.

After Bonnie stops laughing, she gets serious again, "Character snapshots. How are we doing on the character snapshots? You have to make sure you have the story right in your mind so that everything leads to where you are going. Character snapshots define where your characters start and where they are going to end up. You need more guys in this book too."

This is not the first time Steven has heard this advice from Bonnie.

"And social media and branding. We are going to have to start talking about branding and social media."

"I have compiled a list of the top one hundred periodicals and newspapers by circulation, top radio talk shows, top television talk shows, and bloggers. I probably have a list of over five hundred news outlets and media personalities that could be interested in talking about my book. What goes into a press package for all of these individuals?" Steven considers the quantitative goal he set for himself all those months ago.

"Soooooo. Your current headshot, your bio, a summary of the book, the top ten key points in your book, and generally you give a description of the intended audience for the book."

"OK. Makes sense. Next thing…Now that I own this name, *Forty-five is the New Twenty-five*, and no one else can come out with this book, I can start to put posts out there on Facebook to socialize the idea of this book…but if I am being honest, I am afraid," Steven confesses.

"I get it. I understand. Every one of my writers goes through this, and ultimately, they just do it. And none of them are dead yet," Bonnie shares, trying to lighten the mood a little.

"OK. In one week, I will set a goal that I will make one post on Facebook letting people know that this book is coming."

"OK. Have you heard from Stephanie?" Bonnie asks.

"No. I'll email her again once we are through here."

From: Steven Sharp
To: Stephanie Thomson
Subject: I am afraid!

Hey Stephanie,

I have been thinking a lot about you. I have also been working a lot on my book! I have been making a lot of progress. I am getting excited, and at the same time, I am scared! I have to start to think about my book as a product that I must market and it is scary! I have to 100% believe the ideas in this book, and I do, but for some reason I am still scared. It doesn't make a whole lot of sense.

I wanted to let you know I was thinking about you. How is school? When are you graduating? I'd love to hear about your experience in Haiti. Maybe we can grab a coffee if you are ever in Atlanta?

Let me know how you are doing. I miss you.

Steven

Steven grows concerned that he has been ignoring his one true friend in the world to focus on his book project, so he grabs his phone and sends a text to Michele.

> Hey Michele! Hope you are enjoying your summer... Miss you!! Want to hear about how the job search is going. Not now obviously... Going to bed. Let's catch up soon!

A couple of days later Steven receives an email response from Stephanie!

From: Stephanie Thomson
To: Steven Sharp
Subject: Re: I am afraid!

Hey Steven!

Hey!! Don't be afraid. Don't limit yourself. You can do it!!!

School is going very well. It is my last semester here and I really want to be able to spend time with my friends and make the most of being here in Auburn before I move back home. I graduate on December 14th!

I would LOVE to tell you about my experience in Haiti! It was truly life-changing. It makes me appreciate the things that I have so much more because you're around people who have hardly any earthly possessions, yet are full of so much happiness and joy. I try not to complain as much anymore, because compared to them, I have absolutely **nothing** worth complaining about. They do, and they never complain. Sadly, the United States of America has become a very self-centered, entitled society. Being in Haiti was refreshing because there, it is not all about you. You see real hurt and abject poverty. Children who have seen their parents murdered in front of them, devastation from the tragic earthquake a few years ago, people who practice voodoo. It's a different world. And yet, through all the bad, it is so clear that God has brought so much **good** from it. Orphans are taken in and given loving homes and a good education, giving them a hope for a future. People are healed and turn away from their voodoo practices. Hospitals with dedicated workers that take care of malnourished babies all day and all night so that they can become healthy again. Children who live in the slums who are not malnourished due to programs that feed those children every day. It's incredible. And that doesn't even scratch the surface of my experience in Haiti, but that's a little bit about it! I'd love to tell you more sometime.

Miss you too! How is everything going?

Stephanie

Steven thinks about what Bonnie had experienced in Haiti and that she would be glad to hear what Stephanie would say about her own experience in Haiti. He gets down on his knees and places his hands together, "Dear Lord, I pray you allow me to see the world through Stephanie's eyes, to see the happiness and joy despite the abject 'poverties' that exist all around me."

As Steven stands up and opens his eyes, he looks for his tablet so he can send an email to Michele, since she won't reply to his text messages.

To: Michele DiFranco
From: Steven Sharp
Subject: Catching UP

Hey Michele!!

How are you doing? I hope you are doing great. I am doing well. We are having a really rainy, but remarkably cool summer.

I wanted to talk to you a little about my book project if that is OK? I have homework to do for my next appointment with my book advisor. I have to complete a character snapshot of each of the main characters in my book. The character snapshot is simple. It defines where the character starts at the beginning of the book and where the character ends up at the end of the book. This brings up a challenge I have been wrestling with for the "character" of Michele. We started you on this journey of conquering technology and creating a range of career options for you, but then my life, my book, my getting in shape started to take center stage and your three kids got out of school for the summer and needed a full time mom.

So I have been thinking that I haven't been able to support you on your journey toward career independence as I had hoped, and the book will be finished in September, about the time your kids will be back in school. So, just when you would have more time to devote to creating a new future for yourself, the book will be finished.

So I am worried about where Michele's character will end up?!? Will she end up in a place much like where she started? Or will she end up in a place with current computer skills and a range of career options open to her?

Both are OK of course:-). Either would work for the book. Or, we cannot include Michele's character, if that is easier. Not everyone can rise above her circumstances. Even as I type this, my shoulders slump a little and a sadness pervades me. (When I re-read this last night to make sure I wanted to send it to you, I started to cry. I believe in you so much.)

I want your character to be in there. I want her to be the one that proves her naysayers wrong, not one that in certain ways confirms the traits the naysayers believe she embodies. If it is any consolation, I believe you possess everything opposite the naysayers believe about you. You have been lacking a support system to help you overcome the conditioning that has been engrained in you.

The ghetto is in your mind, Michele. The ghetto is in your mind. It is every excuse you allow yourself to make. It is every dream you don't write down. It is the blank goal sheet included with this book you don't take the time to complete. It is every time you have needed help from me and stopped yourself from asking for it.

What shall I put in the character snapshot next to Michele? Let's figure out where will Michele end up? Please email me back with your thoughts on this subject, on your life.

Love,
Your best friend, Steven

Hey Michele!! I sent you an
email... Hope you are ok.

Steven and Dan run and Steven can
have a conversation.

Dan and Steven are on a run, and Steven is actually able to carry on a conversation while they jog – a big change from the usual grunts he musters as Dan carries the conversation.

"I'm afraid, Dan," Steven confesses. "I own the title of my book now, and I can start to let people know this book is coming, and every time I tell myself I am going to make a post to Facebook, I always talk myself out of it."

Steven watches for Dan's facial expression out of the corner of his left eye, while also focusing on the traffic light ahead of them, trying to keep their pace so that they catch the light at the next intersection. Dan takes a quick glance at Steven, and then focuses back on the road in from of them. Dan reaches his arm out and slaps Steven on the back of his shoulder. They run in silence for awhile and then discuss work politics and the next race Dan is training for.

As they return to work, walking the last hundred or so yards back to the locker room, Dan steps in front of Steven, stops and faces him. "Steven, when we first started running together, you couldn't even say your name, let alone carry on a conversation. Look at how far you have come. You talked my ear off this afternoon. You can post to Facebook. I am sure of it."

Chapter 27
...But I Do It Anyway

Meagan Gadreault has been interning with Steven for the last few months. Meagan is very bright, has a mind of her own, and she loves to laugh. Steven would have liked her even if this were all she had going for herself. When describing Steven to her mother, she described him as a "gossip queen," and once Steven heard that, there was no turning back. He L-O-V-E-D Meagan.

After his book advisor started to discuss the importance of social media for promoting his book, and since Meagan lived on Instagram and Twitter, Steven asked Meagan if she would help him set up the pages he needed. Without hesitation, Meagan said yes: No questions asked and no expectation of being compensated. Just a willingness to help. She was also the person most interested in reading a draft of his book. Steven had four unpaid people in his life willing to help him realize his dream of being a published author and getting back in shape: Stephanie, Meagan, Dan, and Michele.

Steven stops for a moment and squeezes his eyes shut. "Dear Lord, please help me to continue to be a person who supports the greatness in others. Help me to be the type of friend that Stephanie, Meagan, Dan, and Michele have been for me."

Not only does Meagan agree to help with the social media, she takes the initiative and sends the following email to Steven.

From: Meagan Gadreault
To: Steven Sharp
Subject: Happy Thursday!

Can you send me what you want for your social media stuff! Like how you would like me to set things up. I am going to create a Facebook page and Twitter page. Also a YouTube channel, but we need to decide a plan of action.

Like what kind of logo do you want to use? How do you want to brand your book? Let me know your thoughts and ideas. I am here to help.

Steven is taken aback by the line, 'I am here to help.' His confidence is gaining momentum. Now that he is gathering support for the launch of his book, Steven musters the courage to post to Facebook:

Steven Sharp

So anyway, I've had this dream for as long as I can remember. I have tried countless times to make it happen. I finally figured out what was missing: a support system that supported a bigger me than I have ever allowed myself to be. The dream? Being a published author. I am 200 pages into a book that will teach you how to have the best years of your life still ahead of you, regardless of your age. "Forty-five (truly) is the New Twenty-five." Stay tuned for the Steven Sharp who is not afraid to use social media to socialize the ideas that comprise my book.

He is not quite here yet, but he is on his way.

Judith Miske Steven that is so incredible!!!

Rosemarie Intile I have always looked up to you as a kid. I look forward to reading your book. You were an inspiration then and now. Love this! Seriously. You are the real deal. People don't change. Go for it!

Leticia Helena Fraga Oprah...are you ready? HE is coming!!!!

Tammy Atwood Honaman Steven - all the best as you complete each new page. May your thoughts remain clear, true and limitless - and may the love and support of those around you keep you going until you finish this thing! From one of your fans

Steven Sharp Tammy, Chip, Leticia, Rosemarie, Judith, you are all so awesome for saying such kind things to me. HUGE thank you!!

Pamela Laurent Sharp, you are one in a million, love that you are making it happen! Miss you! Xo

Kelly Moran Brink I'll buy it.

Julia Scott I wanna read drafts!! Sounds aligned with every Midlife book I ever read, only better. Please do.

Ken Sharp You go man. I remember that protest letter you wrote, don't even remember what it was about. All I remember was it was the most powerful letter I've ever read. You have the gift, go for it

Steven Sharp Awwwwweeee, Ken Sharp, I was nervous about you being my Facebook friend and reading this post. Thank you so much. I love you very much!

Bryan Hawn I LOVE THIS SO MUCH! 200 pages... wow that is amazing! All your thoughts are brilliant... you are so smart and this is a chance for you to use something you are truly gifted at to impact other people. I have no doubt it will be incredible and give people a perspective and new perception that will change their lives.

Steven Sharp Bryan, thank you so much for the encouragement. I am really doing it this time. I was "doing it" when I first met you with my 'wallpaper my way to a new life' technique I had dreamed up to try to write into an existence a me that visited me only in my dreams. Thanks again, Big Bry for the kind words. You look amazing... So I absolutely know you already know what it means to work hard at something. Hope to see you soon. Your friend, Steven

Steven's concern for Michele grows. She's gone days without responding to any of his texts, emails, or phone calls. Steven forces himself to stop imagining the worst.

Steven will be meeting with Bonnie in the morning. He waits until his department is basically empty before printing out the latest version of his 204-page, narrative non-fiction, bestselling book.

He has added a full color cover to the draft and a table of contents. It is starting to look like a real book. He takes the first hundred pages off the printer, looks at the cover, and reflexively clutches it close to his heart. He beams, and hugs *his book* against his chest.

Suddenly feeling foolish, Steven jerks the pages away from his body and wipes the smile off his face. He assumes an air of nonchalance and waits for the rest of the pages to print.

As he's waiting, "Winter" by Tori Amos fills his head.
"When you gonna make up your mind
When you going love you as much as I do
When you gonna make up your mind
Cuz things are gonna change so fast"

Here he is, holding his lifelong dream, wanting both to release it to the world and hold on to it tightly, scared that what he's doing—what he's sharing of himself—might be too painful.

Steven plods forward, his trust in his team and himself helping him overcome his doubts as he gives this copy of his manuscript to Bonnie when they meet at 6:45 a.m. the next morning.

A day or two later, Steven checks his me.com email address and sees an email from Bonnie. The subject line reads, "Comments on 12-20." This stumps Steven. *It isn't December* 20. It *must be some secret book editing code.* Steven excuses himself from his work desk and hurries outside to read her email.

From: BBDaneker@writeadvisors.com
To: Steven Sharp
Subject: Comments on CH 12-20

Hello -

Great job on all the work you've done the past two weeks. I know we have character sketches left to do, but I wanted to record my general comments so we can start tracking. Notice the content comments as well, but no line edits. I'll hang on to those for now. Go ahead and look if you want; we will talk about these later, but I want you to focus on generating more content right now. We will be tying up the threads like we talked about after we nail down the character sketches.

Keep going! We need more content!! Best, BBD

> I read your comments. Does CH mean chapter and 12-20 reference the chapters you have reviewed?

> Yes. Glad you see the connection! See you next week.

Duh. Nice top secret, book editing code. A book advisor referencing the chapter numbers of a book. Ground breaking.

Steven has been calling Michele, leaving message after message. Not hearing back from her is really wearing on Steven. *This is so unlike Michele...Usually it is her leaving me message after message after message.*

Finally a text comes in from Michele.

> I'm OK... my father was in hospital...almost lost foot from complications due to his diabetes. He's OK, just lost half a toe. My Gram has been in and out of the hospital...can't breathe, heart problems, and now cancer. Kids r not in camp n I have to keep them occupied all day...its very hard...I have no time for self...Danny is working all time...I just feel overwhelmed and depressed... hard for me to do my work to prepare to be an instructional designer... I sit at the computer and can't think straight...I have to clear up my anxiety first... I'm sorry if I keep not answering you! You are a good friend! I know you care about me. Worried more and more about my Dad and my Mom and my family...

> Glad to hear from you. Very sorry to hear about your dad and your grandmother. Is there anything I can do to help?

No... nothing to really do... I just need to deal with it and get to a better place... How are you? Is the book going OK?

Well if you want to talk it may make you feel better? I am doing well. Can't complain. Worried about you :-(

I just had a long conversation with your mom!!!!! I called her by mistake when I was trying to call you!! Hope you are OK.

Michele calls him immediately. *How long has it been since they have spoken?* Steven worries that he's trying to force his high achiever mentality onto someone who isn't cut out to be a high achiever. Steven is in the middle of eating dinner at Whole Foods and doesn't answer. He sends a text instead. He will call her later.

From: Aara Parkour
To: Steven Sharp
Subject: Everything happens for a reason, not by a miracle

Hi Steven

I had a thought I would like to share with you that has been on my mind since last night and this morning in my walk... "Forty-five is the New Twenty-five" Your mother might have known the three things she wanted out of life, but what if she knew what more she could do after she became a nurse, got married and had children? At 45, she could have done more but she might not have known given her generation and the traditions in her generation?

You may want to include something like this in your book about raising your level of awareness of the options available to you.

Aara

> Hey SS,
> I hope you are ready for this.
> 19.20% body fat. You are doing awesome. Keep up the good work.

Rather than text Julie back immediately, Steven's first reaction was to text Dan.

> Hi Dan,
> Thank you SO MUCH for helping me get back in shape. I lost a third of my body fat.
> Thanks for putting up with me.
> Your friend,
> Steven

Next, Steven replies to Julie.

> I was not expecting this great of results!! I really can't thank you enough. I was in a huge rut, and I had let myself get so out of shape, this from a guy who was always in amazing shape. Thank you so much, Julie J!!

Steven,
You are the one doing all the work. We can motivate you and push you, but ultimately you are the one that is doing it.
So CONGRATULATIONS to you.
I'm happy to have you as my client and my friend. See you next week - we're not finished with this journey yet - this is just the beginning.
Julie

From: Aara Parkour
To: Steven Sharp
Subject: Thinking about your mom (again)

Good morning Steven,

After I finished my morning prayer, I thought about what your mom (may she rest in peace) again. At 25 – Some of us have been working after graduation and maybe got married – and making an income to raise a family and pay bills. At 45 – is the time when we need to reflect and seek our passion or "our true calling" if we haven't found it before and make sure when we are 70 (another 25 years away) we can reflect back and see how we lived life to the fullest and we may have more years to give and accomplish more.

I used to have hard time taking care of my parents, especially my Dad with Alzheimer's. I felt like I am always giving and not taking care of myself. It was a difficult time. Until one day I was walking at Borders and found this book *29 gifts* and read it and gave me a whole new perspective.

All along I was not giving because if I was giving, I would be asking for a return and I would get frustrated. So I changed my thought process from "I have to do things for my parents" to "I want to give to my parents through the things they need my help with." When I made this mental shift, I started seeing what I am receiving from the little things I hadn't noticed before: my husband smiling at me when he wakes up, my mom helping at home, and my dad telling me he loves me every day.

BTW –

I have been sitting with my mom this morning and having some time together. The morning is her favorite time. Have a wonderful weekend and may all the blessings come your way.

With love,

Aara

From: Steven Sharp
To: Aara Parkour
Subject: Re: Thinking about your mom

Hi Aara,

You are so thoughtful, Aara. If this is the type of person who emerges when you feel connected to someone, you owe it to yourself to connect with everyone you can. For you to listen to a brief little story I shared with you about my mother and to think about it so much, is so unusual and incredible.

People are not like that Aara. They focus on what is important to them, what they want to do, the things they want for themselves.

I love you, too, Aara. I want for you all the great things you want for yourself, and I will do everything I can to help you achieve them. You are doing so well with your mentoring. You are noticeably different. Keep up the work; keep raising your level of awareness. Don't put too much pressure on yourself.

Enjoy the journey as you turn yourself into the person who exists in your dreams.

Love,
Your friend Steven

As Steven clicks send on his iPhone, his mind wanders to Michele and as if on cue, the voice of Vickie Kent fills his head. Steven hasn't seen or talked to Vickie in probably over twelve or thirteen years, but her voice is as clear as if he had spoken with her yesterday, *People don't step up to the plate, Steven. People don't step up the plate.*

At least Michele is answering my phone calls now...Remember, Steven, focus on the things you want for yourself. In the end, that is all you can truly control.

The desire for change has to come from within.

Chapter 28
Food Journal, Food Journal, Food Journal

"I have my food journal," Steven announces as he hands it over to Julie. His journal includes the day of the week, the time he gets out of bed, everything he eats during the course of the day and the times of his meals and snacks.

"OK. I'll take a look at it," Julie picks up her lunch order from the food truck and Steven walks her back to the personal-training-studio-type gym his company has for its employees.

As Steven walks back to his desk from the gym, he thinks, *Julie has been one of the toughest, most-dedicated-to-your-success trainers I have ever worked out with. And I have had at least six personal trainers in my life. Julie knew how important diet is for someone my age, and she wouldn't let me sell out on myself, even if "selling out" was not writing down what I ate.*

Julie was well aware Steven's diet is the reason he's not seeing the results he expects, but she also knows it is something he has to discover for himself. By July 17, for seventeen straight days, Steven had faithfully maintained his food journal. He is honest, thorough, and accurate.

Julie is running a few minutes late for their Thursday morning, 8:00 a.m. workout, "Hey! How are you?" Julie greets Steven. "Hold on, I'll be right with you."

After Julie returns from the ladies room, she proclaims, "Well, I got a real kick out of reading your food journal! I was going through it and I would start cracking up. Kristian was like, 'what are you reading over there?' 'Steven's food journal,' I told him." Julie's blue eyes twinkle and her slight Southern accent becomes more pronounced.

Oh great. Even my food journal is funny.

They workout hard that morning, and Julie even lets Steven do some of his favorite exercises: bicep curls and tricep extensions with the TRx suspension cables and single arm chest press on the stability ball.

As Steven runs up and down the stairs outside of the gym, sweat pouring off him, he thinks about how he used to work out. *These strength-interval, timed-set instead of rep-counting,* straight *trainers do not realize that in the gay world, "No pecs = No sex."* Steven is close to being as fit as he has ever been, but his fitness is realized beneath the surface of his skin this time. It is an internal fitness, a cardiovascular and strength fitness, rather than lots of muscle mass. Muscle mass being what gets you laid on Saturday night in the gay world.

Julie starts to give him feedback on his food journal. "So I want you to know I read every word of your journal and these notes I wrote on the top are a summary of my observations."

"OK."

1. **"Eat at regular intervals.** So I think you did a really good job of writing down everything you ate. On some days, you did great eating every three hours. On other days, your last meal was at 4:30 or 5:00 p.m. or over five hours in between meals. You can't do that. It made me think about your workouts. Some days you'll work out twice or three times in a day and other days you will do nothing. You need to exercise to intensity six days a week, not six times per week. Same thing with eating, you must eat in regular intervals, at regular times. You need to eat meals every two to three hours.

2. **"Food choices.** What kind of ham are you eating? What kind of peanut butter? What kind of cereal?"

"Ham? I have no idea. Peanut butter? Jif," admits Steven.

"Jif has poly unsaturated fat in it. I'm afraid your cereal may have a lot of carbs or a lot of sugar in it."

"It can't. It costs $5.39 and I love it. It's oats and granola. Granola is healthy," Steven claims.

"Yes it is, but granola can have a lot of calories, sugar, carbs, or fat. Why not get some Greek yogurt, use one-third of a serving of granola and five fresh strawberries?"

"Because I hate the grocery store."

"Why do you hate the grocery store?" Julie wonders.

"I don't know…it's huge, bright, takes forever…,"

"Do you want me to go to the grocery store with you?"

"You would do that?" Steven softens and is touched. "For me?"

"Yes. I would do that for you."

3. **"Fruits and Vegetables.** I also wrote down fruits and veggies? Don't you like fruit?"

"Yeah I do, but you have to get that at the grocery store," Steven smiles sheepishly.

4. **"Protein earlier in the day.** You need to eat more protein earlier in the day, like a protein-based breakfast. You need to eat within thirty minutes of getting up.

5. **"Shift proportion of calories you consume.** You need to shift the proportion of the calories you are eating from the end of the day to the beginning of the day.

6. **"Big meals too late at night.** You eat big meals late at night at 8:00 p.m. or later. That's too late. You need to be done eating earlier and maybe have a piece of fruit if you get hungry late at night."

"OK."

7. **"More water.** You need to drink more water. And not like the workouts. A huge glass of water once or twice. Get a huge water bottle and sip from it all day long. You need consistency with your water intake.

8. **"Eating out.** How much do you eat out?"

"All my dinners come from the Whole Foods hot bar."

"OK. When we go grocery shopping together, we will go to Whole Foods too, and we will look at what you can eat, OK?"

Steven tears up, "OK." Snarky Steven has left the gym.

9. **"Empty calories.** The last thing I wrote was empty calories late at night."

"What's an empty calorie?"

"These two glasses of wine, three twenty-ounce Blue Moons, two Texas margaritas...."

"Oh that."

Steven grabs all of the fat around his mid-section and fills his hands up with this cottage cheese-looking skin and fat cells. "I want to get rid of this."

"You see all of these things I wrote on the top of this page? These nine things? That's why you have all of that. If you change these things you will lose the fat."

"These are just minor tweaks though…."

"Yes. I know. That is all you need to do is these nine things I wrote down."

Knowing these small, simple changes to make, he realizes he is getting his diet under control. He feels like he was walking on air as he showers and changes. When Steven returns to the office he announces: "Julie told me it was bad to drink alcohol late at night. I guess I'll have to drink in the morning."

"Oh great," a co-worker replies. "Now Steven is going to blame Julie when he comes to work drunk in the morning."

Chapter 29
When Your Motivation Bucket Is Empty, It Isn't

COACHING PREP FORM

How am I doing today?

> I am doing well. Been sleeping well. Been waking up early
> though and feeling rested. Of course I am not getting up
> immediately, but I am still getting to work by 7:00 a.m. or 7:30
> a.m.

> I have been writing in my book regularly. I actually look forward
> to it now. I really enjoy it too?!? What is going on with me? I
> fight myself so hard, Debby. I'd like to work on this today. Why
> do I make things so hard on myself?

"So, where do you want to start today?" Debby asks.

"Well, what stood out for you?" Steven responds.

"Well, it sounds like you really want to get some resolution around
why you make things so hard for yourself. So let me ask you a
question. What do you get out of it?"

Steven sits silent on the other end of the phone, staring at the wall,
willing an answer to materialize in his mind. Nothing. Crickets.
Steven finally answers, "I honestly don't know, Debby."

"And that's OK. And, that's better than a lot of answers I get to that
question."

Steven asks, perplexed, "What do you think I get out of it? Why do you think I do it? It makes no sense to me."

"A client of mine and I worked through this for several months and we came up with this theory. It goes like this: A person has a finite amount of motivation that resides in a bucket of sorts. Once the motivation has been used to get to work, workout, house work, take care of your children, etc., motivation for the other things you want to do can be depleted. You get to a point where there is nothing left. How does that sit with you?"

"It's interesting. I'd have to think about it. I think it makes a lot of sense, but there is one part that doesn't sit well with me."

"What is that?" Debby asks curiously.

"I agree that the motivation bucket can become depleted or empty, but at the exact same time that you perceive your motivation bucket as empty, it isn't," Steven explains, both thinking out loud and talking to Debby.

Steven continues, "Well if your theory is correct, there should be times when you can never, ever motivate yourself to do something, and that is simply not the case. Motivating yourself to do something is as simple as flipping a switch in your brain. It's changing the music you listen to. It's making a decision."

Steven thinks back to what he wrote in the introduction to this book: *I have realized the simplest choices, the smallest actions, are choices we make to live or die. And, I choose to live.*

"You make a good point, Steven, but sometimes as hard as you try, a person can't flip the switch," Debby counters, as they both realize their time is up for this session.

From: Steven Sharp
To: Michele DiFranco
Subject: Introduction to Aara Parkour

Hi Michele,

The purpose of this email is to introduce you to a colleague of mine. Her name is Aara Parkour. Michele meet Aara. Aara meet Michele.

Michele, I hope you are doing well. I wanted to thank you for being concerned about possibly holding up progress on my book over the summer with all the challenges you have been facing. I can only imagine!! I am glad you made it through it all...

I think your concern demonstrates how much you care about me and my ability to succeed at what I set my mind to do, e.g. this book. So I am sure you can understand that I would have this same concern for you, that you would be able to accomplish the things that you set your mind to, too. In your case, re-enter the workforce after being a stay-at-home mom.

I have reached out to someone I work with named Aara Parkour and asked her if she would help me to mentor you, to provide you with the support you need to rise above the conditioning that has been engrained in you. Aara is an incredibly compassionate, caring, smart, funny, successful business person, and she has agreed to work with me to help you reenter the workforce. Please "reply all" to this message and say the following:

"Thank you. I accept."

I love you very much, Michele. In certain ways, if your life is less than it could possibly be, than my life is invariably less too. Let's do this thing together and show all of the naysayers in your family and in your life that they couldn't have been more wrong about your potential, the things you can accomplish and about you.

I believe in you.

Your best friend,
Steven

Hey Michele!! I just sent you an important email. Please check your email when you have a chance and reply!! Hope to hear from you soon. Miss you!!

Early the following day, Aara sends the following email response to Michele. Michele has yet to respond to Steven via text or email.

From: Aara Parkour
To: Michele DiFranco
Subject: Re: Introduction to Aara Parkour

Steven, - Thank you for the introductions, kind words and sharing some details about Michele's personal life.

Michele, - I am sorry for the challenges you have been facing that Steven alluded to in the email introduction... As Steven said, "I can only imagine!"

Just to share something personal about me, my parents live with my husband and I, and we take care of them as our kids. It is a blessing to have them around with us. We are trying to have our own kids but we are having some challenges at this time. My father has been diagnosed with Alzheimer's and with our faith, love and care for each other, we continue to do the best that we can in order to have another blessed day.

I hope you have a good weekend and it is a pleasure meeting you...you are Steven's dear friend and it is always a blessing to connect with others in our lives.

Aara

After reading Aara's thoughtful, kind email to Michele and getting no response from Michele, Steven grabs his phone and dumps everything on his mind into a text message to Bonnie.

Bonnie,
I don't know what to do about Michele's character. I feel like she is like Haiti in a way. Does a true friend tell her there is devastation all around her or help her to see the things she has to be thankful for? I tried to introduce Aara to Michele, to get them to speak on the phone. On my *island, in my mind*, they did speak. Aara helped me to help Michele focus on her career, and through their communication, Michele discovered Aara is 44 and has been unable to conceive a child of her own. Aara got to feel thankful for her career success and Michele got to feel thankful for her family. BUT IT NEVER HAPPENED, BONNIE. And now my book is due. I have to write the end for Michele's character and I don't know what to write.

Steven,
You have been worried about Michele's character for a long time. Being a juvenile diabetic, it was risky for Michele to have children at all, let alone to have three children. Michele's family is her greatest gift. Not everyone is capable of changing, Steven.

Bonnie,
I don't know if I can accept that, nor if I believe it.

Steven goes straight to Starbucks after work. *I have now written in my book five nights in a row*, Steven thinks to himself, and a surge of pride warms his body. *Is it really as easy as going straight to*

Starbucks in my work clothes as Debby suggested, rather than stopping home first? Please tell me it is not that easy.

While at Starbucks Steven receives an email from Aara.

From: Aara Parkour
To: Steven Sharp
Subject: Paying it forward...

Dear Steven,

Guess what I am doing tomorrow?

Such an awesome opportunity to mentor a group of girls on developing their goals, define their values and also discuss social media etiquette with them....

Thank you for all you have been helping me with...we will catch up next week.....

WOW! Steven thinks to himself, *Aara is already getting closer to one of her goals serving on the board of a non-profit that serves women or children in need.* Steven grabs his phone and fires off a quick reply.

From: Steven Sharp
To: Aara Parkour
Subject: Re: Paying it forward...

Aara,

This is so awesome! I read through all of these documents you attached. The goal setting exercise you led with the girls sounded familiar, didn't it? It makes me so proud that you are already achieving the things that are important to you. Aara, you have been blessed with a very kind, compassionate heart. These young girls are so fortunate to have your mentorship.

Can't wait to hear all about.

From: Aara Parkour
To: Steven Sharp
Subject: Re: Paying it forward...

Steven,

I think this picture says it all.

Thank you for all the help you have given me.

Love,
Aara

Getting this email from Aara reminds Steven he wants to introduce Aara to Bonnie, since Bonnie is so well-connected in the Atlanta non-profit community. Steven emails Bonnie, introducing her to Aara.

From: Steven Sharp
To: Bonnie Daneker
Subject: Intro to Aara Parkour

Hi Bonnie,

I'd like to introduce you to Aara Parkour. Aara is the woman I have been mentoring and she has a long term goal of serving on the board of a non-profit that serves women and/or children in need. I was wondering if we could all meet for lunch one day and I introduce you to each other?

Let me know. Have a great weekend!

SS

Closing: Message in a Bottle

It is 10:32 p.m. on Wednesday evening, and Steven's book is due the next day for developmental editing. On Thursday, Bonnie will review his manuscript one last time. Then, on Monday, the manuscript will be submitted to Melissa Heffner of Second Look Services. Melissa is the editor Bonnie recommends. After Melissa's developmental editing, the book will go to his test readers and then final line editing.

To everyone reading this book, this chapter is a message in a bottle from the island I have lived on while writing this book to the island of your world. An island where I have allowed myself to be the antithesis of everything I ever was in the real world. Inside this bottle, inside this book is a message of hope, gratitude for those who have helped me, and inspiration for those who desire a different future for themselves.

I can no longer put off writing about the "character" of Michele, Steven thinks to himself.

You have to tie up all of the loose ends. You have to delight and satisfy the reader. Steven hears the voice of Bonnie in his head as he looks at his watch and realizes it is after 1:00 a.m.

This book is due *today.*

Michele, you have to stop watching TV after your kids have gone to bed or during the day while they are at school. You need to follow the six simple steps I outline in Section Three, Writing Your Own Book. I'd love to help you if you let me. All you have to do is ask, but you have to ask. I can't force my values onto you. Michele, I encourage you to be thankful for the children you have, and not to focus on the things you've yet to achieve in your life. I do believe forty-five is the new twenty-five, but only if you are willing to do the six things I recommend. If not, forty-five is the same forty-five.

On a final note, Michele, you have been the best, most loyal friend anyone could ask for. You agreed to help me with this book because you have heard me talk about this dream for at least twenty years. Not everyone gets to be a parent in this lifetime. Some people can only give birth to a book....

This book is my message, and in some alternate universe, you are stranded on the island of your life staring out to sea. On the horizon, you see a book in a bottle floating toward you. The bottle beckons you into the water. You start wading slowly, and then paddle furiously out to sea as the bottle floats to within your reach. You grab the bottle, swim back to shore, and break the bottle open. Out pops this idea that you can be anything you want to be, regardless of your age.

You begin to read *Forty-five is the New Twenty-five*, and a part of you that has been dead for a long time begins to awaken.

Before I started writing this book (this time), I was lost. I had no real goals; I had nothing I enjoyed except work; I had gained over twenty-five pounds, had a thirty-seven inch waist and 29.5 percent body fat. I had no hobbies and nothing I looked forward to. I sat in my loft by myself, listening to the songs I had listened to at least a thousand times before, trying to imagine what the latter years of my life would be like. I couldn't really imagine anything good. Today, I sit in my loft in absolute silence, without the distraction of my *Steven Typical Playlist*, pouring all of my thoughts and concentration into this book and determined to make it as good as I can make it at this time.

I created this *place* I am enjoying today when I mustered the courage to write down my goal to be a published author and to rediscover the physique and level of physical fitness I had when I was in my twenties. By writing down these goals, in effect, I identified the things I didn't know how to do: I didn't know how to write a book, to create characters, or to construct a plot; I couldn't motivate myself to work out regularly, and I had no control over what I ate or when I ate it.

However, I didn't let the fact that I couldn't do these things stop me. I found others who knew how to do what I wanted to do and who were willing to help me. For these people, I am eternally grateful.

I liked the idea of starting this book with comparing myself to John Locke from the television series *Lost* and suggesting that this book was like the mysterious island in the show, a haven from the real world where I could be anything I wanted to be, regardless of what I had been before I started writing the book. If you are familiar with the show, you will know that John Locke was wheelchair-bound in "real life" before he landed on the island. Something mystical happened when he landed on the island and his ability to walk was miraculously restored. When I started conceiving of myself as the protagonist of my book, rather than this now forty-six-year-old instructional designer from Atlanta, Georgia, *my ability to walk was miraculously restored.* Where *walking* is being happy with how my body looks and absolutely convinced that the best years of my life lie still ahead of me. In the *book* I am writing, my world is full of people like Dan Chase, Michele DiFranco, Julie Jones, Bonnie Daneker, Amelia O'Connor, Debby Stone, Stephanie Thomson, Bryan Hawn, Cindy Lucas, and Meagan Gadreault: people who are willing to help me accomplish the things I was unable to accomplish on my own.

I have also learned true joy in life comes not from the actual achievement of the goals you set for yourself, but from truly believing your goals are attainable and working toward them on the days you have enough energy. We do not need to be super human to achieve the goals we set for ourselves. We need to be intentional about how we spend our time and make sure the time we spend is invested toward a future state we'd like to achieve.

My life has been different since I began to ask myself, "What would the hero of my book do?" The idea of me being a character in my own book gave me permission to do the things I wanted for myself, but couldn't bring myself to do, or was unable to do. Nobody wants to read a book about a guy who always wanted to write a book and fails in the end. They want to read a book about a hero, someone who has conquered his fears and his inadequacies. For this reason, and maybe this reason alone, I have been successful this time. Because of you, the reader, I have been successful. I wanted you to be able to read about someone who was able to achieve what he set his mind to do.

In so many ways, this precious life we lead is only bound by the things we don't believe we are capable of doing. The ghettos we experience in life exist only in our minds.

And we may be right, we may not be capable of doing the things we dream about, or we may not know how to do them. Not knowing how to do something is not an indication that we cannot or will not ever be able to do it. It is a challenge for us to learn how to do it, to form a team of people who support the person we want to be. To not allow the naysayers to limit what we can become. To identify the ghettos that exist in our minds, the limitations we place on ourselves because of...whatever... the way we were raised, what our parents did or did not do for us, the way we were mocked as a child.

Dreaming has transformed Steven. There is a difference between dreaming and pretending, as Jewel noted in the chorus to her epic song, "Goodbye Alice in Wonderland."

There are no limits to what you can become. You can achieve any one of your dreams you have the courage to dream and to write down. You can lose the weight, find your dream job, learn how to love life again, feel like the best years of your life are still ahead of you.

In Chapter one, "Lost," I asked the question: "As I write this future for myself, is it just that, a *written* future? A 'me' that exists only on these pages? Or, are the things I write about capable of impacting the 'me' who is living and breathing outside this book?"

***

After *Forty-five is the New Twenty-five* comes back from Steven's test readers, Steven and Bryan get together for a Saturday night out on the town, ten days before final line editing. This time, Steven picks Bryan up from his mom's house in Alpharetta. In just ten days, Steven's book will be finished.

"Steven, you look great! Your haircut looks…this is the best haircut I have ever seen on you…ever. It's phenomenal! You look so much younger. What you're writing about in the book is transforming you. You're turning into what you are writing about," Bryan says to Steven as he greets him incredibly enthusiastically.

"Wellllll…I knew if I wrote about it, it would cause the particles in my proximity to rearrange themselves into what I wrote about. Rather than write it into a journal this time, I wrote it into a book. This is a nonphysical law of the universe. I wanted to prove to all of the naysayers, to all of the rational skeptics, that if you write down the recurring thoughts you have running through your mind, they will happen."

"You are so smart, Steven. You accomplished several goals at the same time—your book, your fitness; you've recaptured your youth. It's absolutely working."

***

As Steven finishes typing his closing, he hears his text message alert. Bleary-eyed, he searches for his phone. Once he finds it, he stares down at it as tears begin to stream down his face. *It's happening*; Steven reads Michele's text one last time before heading off to bed.

Steven,
I just finished reading the draft of ur book. SO PROUD OF YOU. It is so inspirational! And, if it's not too late, I do want your help☺

Better reply now, Steven thinks.

Remember: The best time to plant a tree is twenty years ago (when you are twenty-five). The second-best time is now.

It's never too late Michele. I'd love to help!!!

Rather than heading off to bed, Steven stops at his Lenovo touchscreen and searches for "Celebration" by Kool & the Gang. He blares it, dancing around his loft.

Even better than he did that day at Starbucks.

Acknowledgements

Stephanie Thomson, when you get here, consider this: You were the first person who agreed to help me, a forty-five-year-old man you barely knew. You agreed to be my pen pal, and during our correspondence, I got to know a faith-based, youthful, and idealistic young woman who has been "gifted with a mind that can think, hands that can do good, and a heart that can love." I would add to this that you have been given a pair of eyes that are able to see the good in people, the joy, and the love. This perhaps is your greatest gift.

When I shared with you the dream I don't dare myself to dream, you encouraged me to consider that investing in people, providing them with encouragement and words of affirmation, is most certainly love. If these things are love, I'd like to think this book is about love. You have your whole life ahead of you, Stephanie! The two prayers I utter in this book are from a guy who hasn't prayed in a long time. I'd like to think you had something to do with these prayers forming in my mind.

Dan Chase, I know you slowed your pace down by at least a couple of minutes so I could keep up on our runs together. Though I don't know what goes on in that head of yours, I do know that few people can make choices that solely benefit someone else, without there being something in it for themselves. You did not need me to train for your half marathons; you are able to motivate yourself to train. You don't need a running partner, but you were willing to be mine, I can only assume, because I so clearly needed one. I guess this message to you is my official, formal thank you.

Julie Jones, thanks for not giving up on me with my food journal, for being the best trainer I have had, and for helping me to realize the importance of diet. You and your company have the ability to change people's lives. Please come to my book launch party and see the "new me" you helped to create. You said this journey was just beginning for the two of us. I hope so!

Bryan Hawn, you have inspired me more than you know! Your heartfelt posts on Facebook were awesome, your encouragement always genuine, and you provided confirmation that the things I am writing about are the same things other great minds (You!) have already discovered. The last time you were here in Atlanta, you gave me the nutrition advice I needed to reach my goal weight. On page 59, I asked, *Who is giving me the encouragement?* I now have my answer: Bryan Hawn is giving me the encouragement! Bryan, your chapter-by-chapter, incredibly positive feedback was awesome and kept me going.

Vickie Kent, you are by far one of the most influential people in my life. Not sure if you know that or not? You made me feel smart and took me to see *Hairspray* on Broadway, and we sat in the front row! You taught me about grace and how to make someone feel like a valuable part of a team.

Meagan Gadreault, Leticia Fraga, and Cindy Lucas: thank you so much for helping me understand how to use social media to promote the ideas in my book, for creating a kick-ass website, and for helping with logistics for the book launch. I talk about a lot of things in this book: setting goals, career, being intentional. If you ever need help with anything, I'd love to help. All you have to do is ask. I am confident if anyone can help me reach the top, it is you three.

Amelia O'Connor, thanks for nominating me for the character award at work and sharing the process you followed to change careers. Also, for opening up to our readers about the external factors that influenced your career path. And for being someone I always look forward to talking to. You add a lot to my life, and I am thankful you shared your existential epiphany at the coffee machine that day!

Michele, thank you so much for believing in me and not abandoning me during my dark years. You should be almost as proud of this book as I am, because without you in my life, I'm not sure it would have had the focus and relevance that it does. You helped me achieve this lifelong dream more than you know. Know that I'm with you in your years, dark or sunny.

To my current employer, Cbeyond, its founder, Jim Geiger, and Joan Tolliver: some day in a future book you will know how thankful I am that this company exists. For now, a heartfelt thank you for instilling in the veins of this organization a character that is real, gives this organization life, and makes it such an awesome place to work.

Melissa Heffner, my editor, for making sure every comma, semicolon, and quotation mark were in their proper place.

Thanks to Jen Gage-Baggett for the pictures that capture the essence of who I have turned myself into by writing this book. Lee Breed, thank you for designing the book cover I love, for working with me to bring my vision to life and making sure what I wanted did not compromise your superb design aesthetic.

Chris Gorton, the most influential person in my life, I know you are not *in* this book, but the work ethic you instilled in me is. Without this work ethic and what you have taught me, I fear I might still be "just a frustrated dreamer." Thank you for all you do for me, every day, in every way.

Debby Stone, thank you for listening to me so intently during our coaching sessions, for introducing me to a "book advisor" when I wasn't even sure if there was such a thing, for helping me to discover that writing can be fun, for reading every word of my manuscript, offering constructive feedback, and for walking on this journey with me. I am not sure I would feel so light right now without your influence in my life.

Bonnie Daneker, how can I ratchet someone back who has helped me achieve something I have wanted to accomplish my whole adult life? I have learned so much from you about writing!

I have learned how to be a *published* author.

Thanks to Livescribe® and Logitech® for creating such great devices that helped me convert this book from my mind to the written page. It wasn't always easy, but your devices helped me learn to be a better writer.

And finally my father. Dad, thanks for the great advice you have always given me, and for telling me that day on the phone when my motivation was at a low point: "Finish your book, take your time, make it as good as you deserve it to be, and then get it out to the world."

Most of all, thank you for accepting me the way I am; this is not a luxury all gay children can claim for themselves. You make me feel lucky every day.

SECTION 3
Writing Your Own Book

Stephanie Thomson

"You were taught, with regard to your former way of life, to put off your old self, which is being corrupted by its deceitful desires; to be made new in the attitude of your minds; and to put on the new self, created to be like God in true righteousness and holiness."

—Ephesians 4:22

Put off, "I am a failure" and "I am ashamed," and put on, "I am loved by God" and "I am forgiven."

—Stephanie Thomson

[And complete the activities in this book.]

Six Steps to a New You

While learning how to be a published author and reclaim the athletic, in-shape body of his youth, Steven followed these six steps to help him achieve his goals. *Forty-five is the New Twenty-five* teaches you how to achieve your goals, regardless of your age; it will provide you with the inspiration you need to do what you know you need to do.

Follow this six-step process to create a different future for yourself.

1. **Write a short narrative of the person you want to be.** Write about the superstar inside of you (less than a page). Include specific things you see yourself doing, specific actions you see yourself taking. Write in the present or past tense.

2. **Identify your values.** What's important to you? Do you value excellence? Family? Fun? As Debby shared with us, how closely we live our lives honoring our core values determines the level of success we will achieve in life. Achieving material or financial success—when being happy and having fun are your core values—will not bring you a level of peace or cause you to feel successful. Instead, it may make you feel lost and cause you to lose your identity. It did for me. Here is a list of things people value.

Creativity	Innovation	Fairness	Trust
Honor	Love	Faith	Resourcefulness
Respect	Accountability	Spirituality	Support
Integrity	Relationship	Honesty	Justice
Safety	Loyalty	Order	Quality
Truth	Flexibility	Collaboration	Friendship
Strength	Security	Dependability	Caring
Authenticity	Commitment	Humor	Connectedness
Play	Persistence	Excellence	Purposefulness
Peace	Learning	Adventure	Freedom
Courage	Fun	Service	Dignity

Identify the top five values from this list. Construct a work and personal life that honors these core values. Doing so will lead to a greater sense of contentment and happiness.

3. **Write down your goals.** Incorporate the dimensions of a healthy self (Chapter Nine). Modify your narrative in Step 1, if necessary, so your goals and narrative are consistent. Create at least one long-term goal in a minimum of three of the dimensions of a healthy self. Identify the small doable actions/ tasks you have to complete on a daily basis to move toward your long-term goals. Define some milestones you will reach and write these in the interim goal section. Achieve your interim goals as you move toward your long-term goals.

To print out a copy of Steven's goal setting worksheet with directions how to complete it, visit www.45isthenew25.com.

Remember, your goals are not real until you've written them down. They can change. Just because they are your goals today, it doesn't mean they will necessarily be your goals tomorrow. Part of your excitement for living and inherent joy in life is related to the belief that you are moving toward a future state you believe will make you fulfilled. Whether it happens or not, believe it will. Don't just read these paragraphs and this book about this now forty-six-year-old no one. For if you do, this book will be no different than any other resolution you have made and never kept. It will be no different than any other fad diet you have tried or self-help book you have read.

The payoff from this book is not from any enjoyment you may have experienced while reading it, but rather from actually DOING the things it recommends.

4. **Create a daily and weekly schedule that supports the person you want to be.** Block out time in your weekly schedule to invest in your longer term goals.

You may not follow the schedule for a long time. I didn't. But I created the schedule that would allow a 45-year-old man to have the body of a 25-year-old. I ignored the schedule for a long time. More than a year. And when I started following it but wasn't realizing the results I expected, I modified it. And I modified it some more.

Recently, I found out I had decreased my body fat percentage from 29.5 percent to 19.2 percent while losing eighteen pounds. The best news? I ate whatever I wanted, didn't restrict, and didn't hate the exercise I did.

5. **Form a team that supports the person you want to be** (No naysayers). Don't do it alone.

This doesn't mean you need to pay an executive coach, personal trainer, or a book advisor. EVERYONE has an unrealized dream, a "book" they would love to write, a place they would like to visit, an amount of pounds they would love to lose.

Get real with a family member, a close friend, someone from your high school graduating class. Ask for help. Be vulnerable. Admit you are fat, but don't want to be. Find yourself your own Dan Chase. Dan was absolutely free, and I think we kind of became close friends while working out together.

6. **Accept, Learn, Adapt, Change, Modify, and Revise.** Accept setbacks. Start again tomorrow. Move forward. Move toward the person you want to be, even if only a millimeter at a time.

Some part of us believes we have to be perfect to change. And it is simply not the case. I am living proof of that. I went through this period where each time I thought about writing this book I was filled with dread. Now I find myself writing for three or fours hours on end, not wanting to stop. In retrospect, I think my fear of the unknown (not knowing how to write a book) inhibited the joy I now get to experience because I was willing to stick with this dream of mine and do the six things I identify in this book.

Playlists and Your Mood

Think about your local health club with
no music. Zumba classes with no beat for
students to follow, spin classes with no
inspiration for those uphill climbs,
runners on the treadmill trying to eke out
that extra mile with no song "to run 'til
the end of," and no background music to
drown out the clanging weights, grunts, and groans of those trying to
tone up and build muscle. It's tough to imagine.

The experience of music and the health club is fused together in our
brains.

Having no music for when we exercise seems hard to fathom, but we
think nothing about having no music suited for how we live. iTunes,
streaming music, smartphones, tablets, and MP3 technologies allow
us to have instant, portable access to the music we love. We can build
customized, mood-invoking playlists for different times of the day:
mornings to wake up, feel calm and centered; **work** to block out
background noise and allow us to focus; **before bed** to relax us and
induce sleepiness; **weekends** for housework and laundry; and of
course **exercise**—to energize us and help us to complete that difficult
run. In so many ways, we are what we listen to, and having "go-to"
playlists to change our motivation levels and mood can help us
accomplish what we don't feel like doing.

The fact is music affects our mood. When building your playlists, it
might be helpful to create your own version of the following playlists:

- moody and introspective
- high energy
- calm and peaceful
- relaxing, sleep-inducing

Listen to each song in your music library and identify the mood it
invokes in you. Add songs that invoke similar moods to the same
playlist.

This is a great post on Mashable.com that identifies five websites that allow you to build custom playlists that suit your mood. http://mashable.com/2010/05/06/music-sites-mood/

The playlists I listen to most often are:

- **Slow Moody Favorites** (My favorite slow and moody tracks, great for when I am home alone or at work. Artists include: India.Arie, Jewel, Adele, Bruce Springsteen, James Blunt, Kelly Clarkson, Tracy Chapman, Tori Amos)

- **Steven Typical** (Songs I will never grow tired of. My all-time favorites. On some level I don't understand, these songs picked me to like them.)

  1. "Winter" by Tori Amos
  2. "Goodbye Alice in Wonderland" by Jewel
  3. "I Got Money Now" by P!nk
  4. "The Lady of Shalott" by Loreena McKennitt
  5. "What You Never Know" by Sarah Brightman
  6. "Foolish Games" by Jewel
  7. "The Promise" by Tracy Chapman
  8. "Never Alone" by Barlow Girl
  9. "Sober" by Kelly Clarkson
  10. "Irvine" by Kelly Clarkson

- **Great Music** (Combination of high energy and more thoughtful singer-songwriter pieces)

- **House Morning** (Calms me. Music I don't listen to normally, background music. Lots of Jewel, James Blunt, and Adele B-sides, lesser known songs)

- **Upbeat 2011** (All-time favorite high energy dance music through 2011. Great for household chores, when I want to go out on Saturday night but don't have the energy, when I have to do yard work, etc.)

Music has the ability to control our moods, and some believe, to influence our beliefs about how we view the world around us. Be intentional about the music you choose to listen to! Change your mood so you feel like doing what you "don't feel like doing."

Changing Careers and Finding a Career You Enjoy

1. Discover what you enjoy. Walk around Barnes & Noble and see what types of books you pick up. What subjects interest you? Working in a field that interests you will seem less like work.

2. Fantasize. Create your dream job, regardless of the education you would need or attributes you would need to possess. Deconstruct this dream job and isolate what it is about this job that is interesting to you.

3. Make a list of your strengths/likes and weaknesses/dislikes. Show it to your friends, colleagues, neighbors, etc. Ask them to help you fill in any gaps.

4. Have your group of friends help you translate your list of strengths and likes into corporate buzzwords and industry-specific terminology.

5. Ask your friends to help you make a list of professions or possible careers you would enjoy based on your strengths and your likes.

6. Talk to people. Let them know you are interested in new career opportunities. Conduct informational interviews with people who hold jobs in the career you are interested in.

7. Be open to the opportunities that flow toward you. Do not be close-minded.

8. Do a volunteer vacation to see if the career you are interested in is something you would enjoy.

9. Consider an unpaid internship or strategic volunteering to obtain the experience you need to change fields.

Losing Weight

Are you overweight? Do you want to live the rest of your life overweight?

I was never overweight and never owned a scale. My life got gradually more sedentary when I got a new job. One day I went to the doctor and he told me I needed to lose weight. I weighed 196 pounds (I also had 29.5 percent body fat). For a long time, I worked under the premise that if you want to weigh less, you have to exercise more and eat less. So I focused on exercise, crafting my week to include six high-intensity workouts, more weeks than not. I did little with my diet since I was working out so much; I didn't think I needed to. At the end of six months, I had only lost four pounds. Depressing. As soon as I started to do the nine things Julie recommended I do, I lost another eleven pounds. Then I plateaued.

Julie's recommendations were great for getting me to a certain point, and I will go back to what Julie recommends because it is more sustainable. However, it is what I learned from Bryan Hawn about sugar, grains, alcohol, and how he explained it to me that has allowed me to keep losing the fat I have accumulated. I now weigh 175 pounds. Was losing the weight easy? Was it hard?? I don't think it is helpful to label whether the process was easy or hard. If it were easy, 35.7 percent of America wouldn't be obese. If you want to lose weight, I think it is important to raise your level of awareness of what you eat, establish new, sustainable, healthier eating habits, and find exercise you enjoy. If you hate the gym and don't look forward to what you are eating, eventually you will turn back into the fatass you used to be.

1. **Keep a food journal.** Write down everything you put into your mouth for a minimum of two to three weeks. Be honest. Get a couple of people you know who are skinny to review it and ask them for feedback. These people are skinny for a reason. They are conscious about what they eat; they exercise; they burn at least as many calories as they consume.

2. **Get a workout / running partner.** Find exercise you enjoy. Group fitness classes help you build social relationships, get in shape and have accountability. Workout five to six times a week. Get into CrossFit® or yoga. Buy a bike, train for a half marathon. Walk. Take the stairs. Get a Fitbit®. Plan your workouts for the entire week and workout when you plan to. When you miss a workout, you can't make it up tomorrow.

3. **Eat intentionally. Bring your breakfasts and lunches to work.** Plan your meals. Everyone who is thin where I work eats every two to three hours; they bring their food to work every day; they are intentional about what they eat, and they carry a water bottle with them wherever they go. They use their lunch hour to work out and eat lunch at their desk. I used to hate to cook, but I couldn't lose any weight without cooking. I cook fish in a skillet and eat tons of vegetables that come in those microwavable bags. I avoid bread and alcohol.

Book Club Questions

1. What "tree" would you have planted twenty years ago if you had thought about it? What tree would you like to plant now?

2. List the ghettos that you would assume existed at one time in Steven's mind. What thoughts were holding him back? Was Steven able to overcome these limitations?

3. If you were writing a book and you were the protagonist of that story others would be reading about, what future would you write for yourself? What challenges would your hero have to overcome and how would you overcome them?

4. If you could transport yourself into an alternate universe, an *island* of your own making, who would you be on that island?

5. List the people Steven added to his team and the role they played in helping him realize a different future for himself.

6. Who is on your team, supporting you to achieve the things you dream about?

7. What does your Naysayer's voice say to you? How do you counter the naysayers you encounter in your life?

8. What externalities influence the choices Amelia made pursuing a Ph.D. in clinical psychology? Think about yourself for a second. What externalities influence you that conflict (or support) your internal desires?

Anyone can support an author's book release. Help to support the release of *Forty-five is the New Twenty-five*.

1. Buy the book.

An obvious point, sure, but important nonetheless. Naturally, we must buy new copies of books, not used copies, for the sale to "count" and the author to get a royalty. So buy new.

2. Buy the book for others as a gift.

Think of which friends and relatives would enjoy the book/novel. Buy a signed copy for them as either a birthday gift or holiday gift. You get to support your author friend and give cool gifts at the same time!

3. When you actually read the book, read it where people can see it.

5. "Like" the author's Facebook Fan page.

Getting your personal friends to "Like" another friend's page is an easy favor to ask, as it requires no money.

6. Attend the book release party (if there is one) and bring a warm body or two.

This task isn't so much to help the author as it is to help the author's self-esteem. It's lonely to have a book release party or local signing with low attendance. If you already bought a copy, bring that book to be signed.

7. Spread news of the book through your social media channels.

When the author mentions it on Facebook, share the news with your social circles and include a small note about what the book is and spreading the word by saying "My friend got published!" is nice — but it's better to say, "This new book by my hilarious friend is a great gift for dads who are raising daughters. Laugh-out-loud-funny stuff for all fathers to enjoy!"

8. If you have media contacts or know people of influence, arrange a connection.

This is one of the best things you can do and probably the biggest way you can truly influence the life of the book and the success of the author.

If you're married to the cousin of a local news personality, it's exactly that kind of connection that serves as a great introduction between author and TV host. If you know a book reviewer at a newspaper in Boston, say so.

---

cruise ship. After all, don't you find yourself looking at what others are reading when you pass by? I do! It's all about building public knowledge of something to the point where people are curious and discuss it.

4. Leave a review on Amazon or BN.com or Goodreads or all.

Reviews are still very important. Think about it. If you come by a new book and see it has 2.0 stars on Amazon, would you buy it? On some level, that silly rating does affect me and my decision — and my guess is that it affects you, too. So it's crucial that, when you read a book and enjoy it, you leave a review on Amazon or BN.com or Goodreads or all. Those first 10-20 reviews really matter and can set a book on the right path. (Note: You can leave the same review on all sites to save time.)